Ideology versus Science:
Climate Change Denial

Dr. William R McPherson Ph.D.

For Jessica, Anna, Lina, and Theo

Contents

CHAPTER 6:
CLIMATE DENIAL AND SOCIAL CHANGE: A PERSONAL VIEW

Preface

Climate change denial is not about conservatives versus liberals, Republicans versus Democrats, or business versus environmentalism. It is about ideology versus science. *It is essential to view climate change denial as ideology to understand its raison d'etre. This book is based on the distinction between ideology and science.*

The science is straightforward and concise: greenhouse gases, such as carbon dioxide, trap heat in the atmosphere. With the advent of widespread fossil fuel use 250 years ago, human activities have increased greenhouse gases from 270 parts per million (ppm) to 400 ppm today. Stabilizing climate requires limiting greenhouse gases. More than 97% of climate scientists agree on this. All of the major scientific bodies in the world also endorse these findings.

Why doesn't 97% of the public agree on the science? Fear of the actions required to reduce greenhouse gases is pervasive, and there are many who would not like to face this reality. They are advocates or followers of denial ideology.

When people deny reality, their ideas can range all over the map. Climate change denial ideology is confusing and diffuse. Is it true belief or propaganda? Many politicians promote it; they may be true believers or not. Propagandists and apologists for fossil fuel industries play a major role, but whether they believe in the ideology or not they are paid shills. Some of the public believes the propaganda for reasons that include expediency and intentional disbelief. All of this requires further analysis because of its implications for the future.

An existential issue of our time is the role of climate change denial ideology. By denying the science, the ideology delays and harms effective action. Understanding this threat requires scrutiny of the conflict between ideology and science. There are scientific findings with which denial ideologues take issue, and those disputes lead to doubts (chapter 1). Organizations supporting denial ideology provide rationales for these doubts (chapter 2). Some of their underlying arguments involving ethics, growth, capitalism, and social change lead to further doubts (chapter 3). These arguments affect American politics in statements by politicians that reflect denial ideology (chapter 4). Political conflict over climate change tends to magnify culture conflict, making resolution of climate issues more difficult (chapter 5). I wrap up all these considerations with some personal views on political and ideological conflict over climate change (chapter 6).

Any discussion of climate change denial begins with examination of the disconnect between science and social responses. Inertia is a partial explanation, because there is often a lag between scientific knowledge and a society's response—for example, smoking and health. But inertia is not a sufficient explanation. A complete understanding of climate change denial requires analysis of the organizations that promote denial. They are the organizations that stand between science and society. They deny the scientific consensus, and scientific consensus by itself is not a sufficient basis for social consensus. It is often mediated by social groups. Although scientists have repeatedly, during the past quarter century, warned us about the risks of climate change, the public has generally regarded the issue as a low priority problem. Polls have indicated that as little as 0.25% of Americans view climate change as a top priority.[1] It would be the highest priority for all Americans if they understood the risks.

More ominously, propaganda by climate deniers in recent years has eroded public acceptance of the credibility of climate science. The press reported a drop in public acceptance of scientific evidence of as much as 20 points in the United States, United Kingdom, and Germany prior to 2011.[2] This has rebounded recently, after record droughts in 2011 and

2012 and Superstorm Sandy, but it is well below the level necessary to pressure a recalcitrant Congress. It is still below the level 15 years ago, before denial ideology became prominent.[3] In comparison, Europeans tend to see it as a high priority issue. More than half indicated that they consider climate change a serious problem, and a fifth said it is the most serious problem facing the world.[4]

Americans are unlike other societies, including our close neighbors, in the degree of uncertainty and doubt about climate change. Canadians are 22% more likely than Americans to say there is "solid evidence" of global warming. Canadians are half as likely to disbelieve the evidence or indicate doubt.[5] The environment minister of Quebec, Pierre Arcand, said, "We don't have sceptics in Quebec. Even on the right, there's a consensus on the need to fight climate change."[6]

A more relevant statistic is how much priority people put on solving climate change. People tend to focus on near-term problems, putting off concern about the longer-term problems where symptoms are not immediately evident. Most Americans rank climate change below most other problems, including jobs, the economy, immigration, and other issues. Less than 1% said that it is the top priority issue.

A compelling finding of public opinion pollsters is that Americans think that the seriousness of global warming is "generally exaggerated."[7] They may be reacting to claims by the denial movement that the science is not valid. Some may think that there is no warming, or if it is occurring it is not serious enough to worry about. Others may support the scientific finding that there is climate change, but its effects are so remote that they need not be concerned now.

I worry about the future of American citizens, especially those who are teenagers now. They will be the ones likely to suffer some of the severe consequences of climate change, such as prolonged drought, heat waves, and superstorms. Fewer teenagers than adults say that global warming is happening or think that scientists agree that global warming is happening. Less than half understand that emissions of cars and trucks contribute to global warming.[8] They are the ones who will have to deal with the consequences of global warming.

I understand that people don't want to think much about global warming. After all, it is a problem that seems remote in time and space: remote in time, because the more serious consequences are likely to occur in the distant future, and remote in space because some of the harshest effects will be in far-off lands, such as Bangladesh and Somalia. It is also a difficult topic to handle emotionally. Many Americans confronted with climate science findings "may experience any number of emotional reactions: fear, guilt, anger, defiance, a desire to blame someone, powerlessness, despair, a sense of exhaustion or annoyance at having to hear the litany one more time."[9]

Wouldn't it be great if someone could give us a way out? Well, someone has. The denial organizations discussed in chapter 2 have exploited the feelings of frustration and anxiety that come from facing facts about climate. While some observers may think that people are just not well informed, the fact is that most are knowledgeable but just don't want to face facts.[10]

These tendencies among Americans are not due to scientific "illiteracy," or lack of knowledge of climate science. Americans actually score better than Europeans on "civic science literacy," but are less likely to be convinced of the reality of global warming.[11] Americans, including Tea Party followers, consider themselves more informed than Europeans about climate science. They also reject climate science findings at a higher level of denial. There is more at work than just lack of knowledge. There is a "culture conflict" that leads many to dismiss climate science. (More in chapter 5.)

It is ideology, not lack of knowledge, that makes denial believers more likely to deny climate science, regardless of their education or status. Climate change provokes some intense feelings because it has dire consequences. It is often easier to ignore the science than to face up to the feelings.[12] Ideology encompasses many emotional themes—personal responsibility, state intervention, regulation, and resources. Analysis of denial ideology will be the main focus of this book.

For purposes of this analysis, I define *ideology* as fixed beliefs about a changing reality. The changing reality in this case is climate. The beliefs are fixed because they are not subject to what Karl Popper calls "falsifiability," the true test of scientific logic.[13] That is to say, ideology depends on beliefs that cannot be challenged with the usual scientific tests of validity.

Chapter 1.
Climate Research, Critics, and Ideology

Scientists don't have fixed beliefs when doing research on climate. Unlike critics who start from the premise that there is no human influence on climate, scientists keep an open mind on the causes and consequences of climate change. They have made a number of important findings about the climate that have drawn attention from denial ideologues.

The empirical basis for climate science is well documented. Scientists have known for over 100 years that increases in carbon dioxide (CO_2) cause increases in global temperature. Svante Arrhenius, the Swedish Nobel-winning scientist, calculated the increase and said in 1906: "The slight percentage of carbonic acid in the atmosphere may, by the advances of industry, be changed to a noticeable degree in a few centuries." He used "carbonic acid" as a label for CO_2.

The leading international organization for the scientific investigation of climate change is the Intergovernmental Panel on Climate Change (IPCC). Since the United Nations Environmental Program and the World Meteorological Organization organized it in 1988, IPCC has prepared five assessment reports based on climate research by thousands of scientists. Each report has analyzed the effects of greenhouse gases (GHG) on average global temperature, as reported by thousands of weather stations. The IPCC's most definitive statement on global warming identifies anthropogenic, i.e., human-induced, GHG as causes of global warming: "Most of the global average warming over the past 50 years is very likely due to anthropogenic GHG increases and it is likely that there is a discernible human-induced warming averaged over each continent."[14] In its recent assessment report, released in 2013, IPCC emphasizes the human role in climate change: "Human influence has been detected in warming of the atmosphere and the ocean, in changes in the global water cycle, in reductions in snow and ice, in global mean sea level rise, and in changes in some climate extremes. This evidence for human influence has grown since Assessment Report 4 (AR4). It is *extremely likely* that human influence has been the dominant cause of the observed warming since the mid-20th century."[15] The term *extremely likely* means the findings are significant to the 95% level.

IPCC findings depend on models, sometimes called Global Climate Models or GCM. Denial advocates attack these models, but they are an essential part of climate science. Although models have their limitations, the scientific process by which they are used ensures that results are checked and rechecked through replication.

Graphs from the IPCC Assessment Reports show the trends in average global temperatures. The graphs, sometimes labeled "hockey sticks" because of their shape, show sharp rises during the past decades (the hockey stick "blade") after a 1,000-year trend of relatively stable temperatures (the hockey stick "shaft").[16] As we will see later, these sharp rises are associated with projections of higher temperatures and other effects of climate change, including droughts, floods, and extreme weather. Skeptics who attribute them to Michael Mann, a climatologist at Pennsylvania State University, have criticized some of these graphs,[17] but many other scientists have confirmed them with extensive research.[18] Congressman Sherwood Boehlert (R-NY) "whose panel in 2006 investigated…charges by climate skeptics that Dr. Mann had falsified results but found no evidence of wrongdoing."[19] The National Science Foundation also cleared Mann of wrongdoing, stating that there was no "evidence of research misconduct."[20] Pennsylvania State University, where he now teaches, has also cleared Mann.[21]

Many denial advocates have challenged the Mann research. Congressman Paul Ryan, vice-presidential candidate in 2012, dismissed Mann's research as "statistical tricks to distort their findings and intentionally mislead the public on the issue of climate change."[22] Most of the criticism of the "hockey stick" is quibbling with the methodology and statistics, attempts to obfuscate the documented conclusions that global warming is accelerating. Often the criticisms are coupled with specious claims that the world is cooling.

One of the most influential reviews of this work was the Berkeley Earth Surface Temperature (BEST) project, which physicist Richard Muller headed and Koch Industries funded. Muller was considered a climate skeptic, but unfortunately for denial ideology, his findings confirmed Mann's research. As Muller has said, "When we began our study, we felt that skeptics had raised legitimate issues...Our results turned out to be close to those published by prior groups. We think that means that those groups had truly been very careful in their work, despite their inability to convince some skeptics of that."[23] Muller's work has confirmed the findings of Michael Mann and many other climate scientists. The globe is not cooling; nearly all of the record high temperatures have been in the past 15 years.

Michael Mann has responded to attacks on his work as follows: "These attacks, they don't represent the feelings of actual people," he said. "They are so-called 'AstroTurf' organizations that will bus people in to try to create the false appearance of grassroots support."[24] He says that the "AstroTurf" organizations are purported grassroots organizations that are actually funded by wealthy individuals or companies (such as the Koch brothers and Koch Industries). Hence the term "AstroTurf," suggesting artificial grass. Organizations such as Americans for Prosperity try to mobilize people to attack climate science with misinformation generated by well-oiled "experts" and think tanks, many examples of which will be found in this book.

Mann expanded his response to attacks to address those inflicted on climate science in general. "The hockey stick's prominence in the climate change debate would secure its status as a principal *bête noir* for those who denied the importance or even the existence of climate change...in the hope that somehow they might discredit all of climate science, the fruit of the labors of thousands of scientists from around the world, by discrediting us and our work."[25]

Another scientist whose work is under constant attack is James Hansen, former director of the National Aeronautics and Space Administration's Goddard Institute for Space Sciences. His work is the target of a number of critics, who assail him for exaggerating the effects of climate change, but his conclusions are solidly based on extensive research. Hansen has done research on a number of effects of climate change. A particular concern is sea level rise, affected by both ocean temperature (warmer water has greater volume) and ice sheet disintegration, which have been associated with higher sea levels in the past. The sea level has already risen sufficiently to cause destructive storm surges during Hurricanes Katrina and Sandy. In the future it may be even more destructive: it can rise as high as 80 feet and inundate the residential and agricultural areas supporting a billion people.[26]

Hansen puts his finger on one concern of climate science: that the warming of the planet will lead to feedbacks such as melting of the ice sheets, which cannot be reversed once they set in. This phenomenon, sometimes called "runaway" climate change, means that policies become more urgent than some projections of changes suggest.[27]

His research has led Hansen to call for strict limits on emissions coupled with plans to bring the amount of greenhouse gases (GHG) in the atmosphere down to a level of 350 parts per million volume (ppmv) of carbon dioxide, a limit that would keep warming within 1°C above levels in the year 2000. At present, CO2 is at 400 ppmv. Hansen's analysis indicates that removing CO2 from the atmosphere would be necessary along with emissions limits.

James Hansen has drawn a lot of criticism because of some of his activism as well his scientific findings. In August 2011 and February 2013, Hansen demonstrated at the White House against approval of the Keystone XL pipeline from the tar sands of Canada to Texas. The demonstrations resulted in Hansen's arrest. Hansen is objecting to the mining of the tar sands, which contain vast amounts of carbon. He has said that if the oil in the tar sands is refined and used, it's "game over" for forestalling climate catastrophe. The Keystone proposal, promoted by Republicans, also drew a sharp comment from Rep. Henry Waxman:

"Many of us believe that that pipeline will lock us into 50 to 100 years of dependence on the dirtiest source of oil that can cause enormous increases in greenhouse gases and lead to greater global warming and climate change."[28]

Keystone XL is a symbol of the main issues of climate change. If we are to continue extracting and transporting large amounts of fossil fuels, such as oil and coal, we are setting the stage for major changes in the earth's climate. Many scientists think that it will be necessary to keep most of the remaining fossil fuel reserves underground to prevent the more serious consequences of climate change.[29] Keystone XL also elicits some of the arguments used by denial ideologues. A spokesperson for the American Petroleum Institute argued that State Department approval of the project "is one step closer to unleashing thousands of jobs that will benefit labor workers, who ave some of the highest unemployment in the country."[30] Job creation is an argument often used by denial ideologues (see chapters 3 and 4), but advocates do not acknowledge that the jobs created would lead to much higher unemployment when consequences of climate change damage economies. An example is the closing of a Plainview, Texas, meatpacking plant after ranchers found they could not maintain herds of cattle during two years of extreme drought. (Details in chapter 4.)

Major scientific bodies, such as the US National Research Council (NRC), part of the National Academy of Sciences, have verified climate science findings. The George W. Bush administration asked the NRC to evaluate the science of climate change and, contrary to expectations, the NRC found that there was robust validity in the findings. As its methodology, the NRC made a broad survey of climate science and reported that greenhouse gases from human activities have risen substantially since the beginning of the Industrial Revolution.[31]

One of the scientific findings the NRC used to reach its conclusions was "climate sensitivity," or the level of temperature increases to be expected from higher concentrations of CO2 and other greenhouse gases. NRC has charted this according to the amount of carbon emissions in the atmosphere. NRC projects temperature changes in ranges between 1°C and 5°C based on the cumulative emissions of greenhouse gases. If, for example, the amount doubles, temperature will increase by about 2°C; if it triples, about 3°C, and so forth.[32] This concept of climate sensitivity has been a bone of contention for contrarians. Some claim that the doubling of CO2 will have little effect, the tripling even less effect, and so forth.[33] One report from the Heartland Institute (see chapter 2) claims: "The IPCC ignores mounting evidence that climate sensitivity to CO2 is much lower than its models assume. Empirical tests of climate sensitivity to increasing atmospheric CO2 indicate negative feedbacks predominate and associated warming is likely an order of magnitude less than the IPCC projects."[34] Such claims are based on an alternative interpretation of the "greenhouse effect" and posit a diminishing ability of CO2 molecules to trap heat and diffuse it in the atmosphere. Most scientists do not acknowledge these claims.

Effects of temperature increases can be severe. The NRC has projected that temperatures will become extreme as a result of carbon emissions expected during the 21st century. Some of the current records for high temperatures may be broken, and hot spells will tend to be longer in the summers.[35] These projections are based on the relationship between carbon dioxide and temperature, a physical-chemical relationship that John Tyndall and Svante Arrhenius established in the 19th century. Nearly all of the scenarios developed by climate scientists use this relationship or analysis of greenhouse gas emissions.[36] As we repeatedly see, this is a major finding of climate science challenged by the critics, who also tend to reject the scenarios based on the relationship.

One of the effects of increasing temperatures is more extreme weather. The World Meteorological Organization, which collates data from all over the world, has observed that it is unusual to have as many extreme events all over the world as we have had in recent years.[37] Extreme weather is associated with extreme denial as ideologues scramble to try to explain away the effects of climate change.[38]

A crucial climate science argument that debunks denial ideology is that increases in temperature cannot be explained without accounting for the role of anthropogenic greenhouse gases. Climate science models have been tested against temperature records, and those models will not work without anthropogenic factors built into them.[39]

One of the most important extreme events in terms of human survival is drought. Drought has already affected the United States, Africa, and China, and it will probably become a more severe effect of climate change in the near future. Referring to recent droughts in agricultural areas, Abdolreza Abbassian, a senior economist with the UN Food and Agriculture Organization (FAO) and a leading UN agricultural expert, noted: "We've not been producing as much as we are consuming. That is why stocks are being run down. Supplies are now very tight across the world and reserves are at a very low level, leaving no room for unexpected events next year. With food consumption exceeding the amount grown for six of the past 11 years, countries have run down reserves from an average of 107 days of consumption 10 years ago to under 74 days recently."[40]

It is not only models and scenarios that show human influences; scientists have also used past data to show that temperature anomalies, i.e., variations from expected temperatures, have already occurred. This research shows that measured temperatures during the 20th century have risen more than would be expected from natural sources.[41] Measured temperature instead matches the temperature ranges expected from human influences.

Research such as these studies shows the trends in climate over decades. Measurement of weather is a much more short-term exercise. It is important to understand the difference.

Weather versus Climate

Many people have confused weather and climate. A friend asked me, how can we believe the experts about global warming when last winter was so cold and snowy? The family of Senator Inhofe (R-OK) built an igloo near the capitol building and stuck a sign on it, "Al Gore's new home," when a major snowstorm hit Washington, DC. Both of these examples show that many people confuse weather and climate. A good metaphor for how to separate the two is "weather is your mood, climate is your personality."[42]

Climatologists and meteorologists agree that weather is measured by days and weeks, while climate is a matter of decades and centuries. Heidi Cullen describes the link between weather and climate change as an issue of timing. Seasons, for example, are changing—spring is coming earlier, and fall is lasting longer.[43]

Although global warming will affect future weather, it is not possible to predict climate on a daily or weekly basis from current trends. The overall trends toward higher average temperatures, increased storm intensity, and extreme weather events are already clear. Whether any one day will be hot or cold, wet or dry, or under assault by extreme storms is not the issue. The issue is the overall effect of climate change on the environment of the future.[44]

Meteorologists and climatologists (sometimes the same people) use models. A local weather forecaster will use models of atmospheric circulation—cold fronts, warm fronts, clouds, and temperatures—to predict the weather for the weekend. A climatologist may use models to predict the next decade or century. Some denial ideologues accuse climatologists of using defective models, or regard any use of models as illegitimate. This does not stop them from relying on meteorological models for planning their weekend based on a weather forecast.

Scientists often have difficulty communicating the implications of climate change in a way that laymen can understand. Many laymen, for example, treat cold weather and snow as evidence that global warming is not happening. This sometimes feeds into denial ideology as proponents use near-term weather to raise doubts among laymen about long-term climate. If these laymen are apprised of the longer-term implications, they can be informed of the ultimate effects of climate change. As Cullen suggests, there is a direct connection, for example, with real estate:

> I can honestly say that real estate is what comes up most often when I talk to people about global warming. While I've spent much of my research career looking at

the global impacts of climate change, I fully understand that people want to see the local impacts. If people are going to understand what is really at stake, scientists have to find new ways to communicate the science, using data, images, and computer scenarios that convey more completely what climate change really looks like—both now and in the future. Beachfront property is only the tip of the iceberg.[45]

Cullen puts her finger on one of the principal problems facing climate science: communication of findings to the public in a way that people understand.[46] As we shall see, criticism of climate science depends on the complexity and uncertainty of some of the findings, which is inherent in the science but not always useful for policy decisions. Criticism also depends on raising doubts about the science, doubts that are exacerbated by the confusion between weather and climate.

Cullen is among a group of meteorologists who have made a transition from "weathermen" to interpreters of climate change for the public. Many meteorologists are in key positions for explaining climate science and have an interest in doing so.[47] Although they indicate that they would like to report on climate change, they are often unable to do so. Research indicates that only 14% of mass media reports on weather issues refer to climate change.[48] Some media, such as Fox News, usually mention climate change only to dismiss it; they deny the role of climate change in any weather issues.

One reason that weathercasters report on climate change less frequently than they would like is because of doubt. Weathercasters are subject to the same denial influence as the general public, and some of them have rejected climate science: "Almost half (47%) felt they needed some or a lot more information before forming a firm opinion about global warming, and almost one third (30%) said they could easily change their mind about global warming. Just over one quarter (27%) agreed with the statement by a prominent TV weathercaster: 'global warming is a scam.' "[49]

It is amazing that one fourth of meteorologists would agree "global warming is a scam." The "prominent TV weathercaster" mentioned in the quote is John Coleman of KUSI-TV in San Diego. He is quoted on the station's website: "We're talking about the greatest hoax in history, let's understand this. There is no man-made global warming. The whole thing is a phony call for quick action."[50] While Coleman is an exception, he does typify the problem: doubt infuses meteorology because of the influence of denial ideology.

Meteorologists doubt climate scientists because of reinforcement of their views by "experts" such as Roy Spencer. He asserts that meteorologists are suspicious of climate models because the climate scientists are disdainful of meteorologists.[51] Spencer asserts that meteorologists have more skepticism about climate than climate scientists. He regards "natural climate change" as a counter to anthropogenic global warming and attributes the skepticism of meteorologists to their rejection of man-made global warming.[52]

Spencer exemplifies ideologues who attribute global warming to natural causes and deny that there are human influences on climate. He incorrectly states "a majority of TV meteorologists do not believe the claim that global warming is man made."[53] His view of the IPCC is that it is composed of "scientific elitists" whose research consists mainly of models, despite the fact that many climate scientists use observations to confirm current warming trends. Nevertheless, his views and those of other denial ideologues tend to influence meteorologists, who then raise doubts about the scientific consensus on climate change.

A more extreme view of scientific treatment of "natural climate change" appears in a book by Spooner and Carter. They assert that "the restricted objectives of both the IPCC and the UNFCCC [United Nations Framework Convention on Climate Change] have caused the United Nations and its scientific advisers to show little interest in the reasons for, and the possible extent of, natural climate variability." They go on to argue that neglect of natural causes distorts the science: "It is easy for bias to develop in such circumstances, wherein all changes that cannot be unequivocally assigned to another cause become attributed to carbon dioxide."[54] It is absurd to argue that the IPCC and the UNFCCC have little interest in natural climate variability. This variability is the baseline against which they measure anthropogenic climate change, so the scientists who contribute to the IPCC assessments used by the UNFCCC have to take into account natural climate change. To suggest that bias will develop in such circumstances is completely beside the point that measurement of human influences has to be made in comparison to natural climate variability.

Again, we see the effect of denial ideology on skeptical meteorologists, even those who are knowledgeable about climate science. More than 60% say there is a lot of disagreement among climate scientists, which is not true, and almost 80% think it is necessary to have a balanced presentation of climate science. This misunderstanding pervades journalistic reporting of climate science and stems from the efforts of denial movements, such as Heartland Institute, to promote alternative explanations of climate change based on invalid science. Meteorologists need to address this misunderstanding in their weather reports. In fact, more than 97% of climate scientists who publish peer-reviewed reports agree that there is human-induced climate change.

Record heat in 2011 and 2012 led many people to suspect that global warming was having an effect on weather. Meteorologists did not explain the link, and many attributed the hot spells to natural causes.[55] Research by Hansen et al. on heat waves has been subject to some criticism, but it has raised questions about whether traditional meteorological explanations are sufficient. Rather than ignoring the role of climate change, meteorologists should examine temperature anomalies, such as these heat waves and droughts, for patterns of climate change. These possibilities should be reported with the weather to provide better public understanding of the relationship between weather and climate.

Despite the efforts of scientists to provide information on climate in relation to weather forecasts, confusion still reigns. This leads people to regard climate change as natural and weather as identical to climate. They then assume that nothing needs to be done to avoid the consequences of climate change.[56] Denial ideologues sometimes take advantage of this confusion and use the supposed cyclical nature of climate to justify their denial statements. As we saw in the previous section, treating climate change as "natural" does not track accurately with temperature trends; only when human influences are included does the trend coincide with measured temperatures.[57]

Perhaps the most egregious misuse of weather to describe climate is *Climategate*, a book based on leaked e-mails and a collection of canards about climate science.[58] The author, Brian Sussman, uses a list of heat records to prove that 1930–1940 was the hottest decade on record, and a list of cold, snowy incidents to prove that the global temperature is now cooling. His claim is rebutted by data in the United States[59] and worldwide[60] that show that the decade 2001–2010 was the hottest on record. He dismisses most of the data used in climate science as "corrupt." He calls climate scientists "whiners" and advocates of climate policies "goons" and "loons."

Another denial ideologue who uses weather records to "disprove" climate science is Sen. James Inhofe of Oklahoma. Although many of Inhofe's constituents disagree, he continues to maintain his denial despite the droughts that have plagued Oklahoma.[61] Inhofe also uses weather records to "prove" there is no global warming.[62] He is a bit less pejorative than Sussman; instead of "whiners" and "goons," he uses terms such as "Hollywood elite" and "antisovereignty internationalists." Internationalism may, in fact, be the only method of addressing climate change, but it does not mean "antisovereignty."

One reason for the disconnect between science and society, described in the preface, is the confusion of climate and weather. "While scientists focus mainly on the broad parameters of climate change and are increasingly convinced of their reality, the direct experience of most people is much more diverse and discontinuous, and the public and media are often diverted and distracted by short-term and local weather events."[63]

It is difficult to get public acceptance of climate change findings when people are distracted or misinformed by the misuse of local weather reports. The use of cold spells, blizzards, and other specific weather events to deny climate science is the most egregious example of this.[64] Politicians take advantage of the confusion of weather and climate. Senator Rubio (R-FL) infamously stated in his response to President Obama's 2013 State of the Union address, "The government can't control the weather." This implies that government has no role in climate change policies, but control of the weather is not the immediate aim of these policies. They will not affect today's weather, but today's policies will definitely affect the weather in 2050.[65]

One way to get people to understand climate change is insurance costs for storms, floods, and other problems involving climate change. Weather-related losses are rising, with estimates running from $18 billion to more than $50 billion in recent years. A large reinsurance company, Munich Re, has named climate change "its biggest challenge."[66]

Some insurance companies have already changed their business plans because of climate change, e.g., Allstate has stopped insuring property in some areas subject to hurricanes. As the effects become expensive to businesses, climate change will become an issue in corporate boardrooms and stockholder meetings. Denial ideology is not an option for business. One insurance executive, President Frank Nutter of the Reinsurance Association of America, put it succinctly: "Insurance is heavily dependent on scientific thought. It is not as amenable to politicized scientific thought."[67]

Risk management is a particular concern of business. Nowhere is this more salient than for the "reinsurance" business, those companies that back up retail insurance companies and provide them with reserves for major claims.[68] "Precautionary approaches" are particularly necessary in insurance businesses. While some have scoffed at the "precautionary principle" that was developed at the Rio Summit in 1992, the insurance industry does not take it lightly. With regard to climate change, the precautionary principle means that companies cannot ignore climate science even if large segments of the population do. Insurance executives and analysts understand the effect of extreme weather on their business.

Unfortunately, many people who understand the need for insurance for private possessions and personal health do not understand the concept at a global level. Reduction of greenhouse gas emissions would be the equivalent of insurance for the entire globe.[69] One could think of climate policies as insurance policies against extreme weather. With regard to the extreme weather events in recent years, climate scientists may not link any one event to global warming but caution that such events are part of a pattern that indicates climate risk.

Insurance companies are reorienting their approach to risk away from insuring weather-related and sea-level perils, especially in coastal regions. The broader concept of risk management would be to require "assurance bonds" for environmental damage.[70] This approach illustrates the role of ecosystem services such as water filtration or flood prevention. The concept of ecosystem risk is still foreign to many Americans. Linking it to the role of insurance would help Americans understand the concept of climate risk. Risk management is the key concept that links climate change to policies such as mitigation (e.g., renewable energy) and adaptation.[71] Risk management depends on the observation of trends as much as individual events.

"Risk management" is another way of saying that societies must adapt to climate change through policies and practices that take account of climate science. As we will see later, there are various reactions to the risks posed by climate change that impact denial ideology. Most of them begin with criticisms of climate science, some more legitimate than others.

Criticism to Ideology

Many critics have addressed the issues raised by climate science. These criticisms can take two forms: skepticism or denial. The skeptics perform a useful service by questioning the data or analysis and spurring scientists to refine and improve their work. Deniers seek to refute the science entirely, either by disputing the data or attacking the scientists and their analysis.

Ashutosh Jogalekar provides a useful distinction, listing three points that help define the difference: "(1) The climate is warming; (2) This warming is unprecedented and is almost certainly because of human influence; (3) This unprecedented warming is going to do some very bad things." He argues that no true skeptic argues with the first, that few argue with the second but most would agree with it, and that there can be honest skeptical argument with the third point.[72] The criticism of skeptics that slides into ideology is the denial that there is human influence on the environment. Denial of this influence depends on belief, not science.

As criticisms move further away from the science, they tend to become ideological. In other words, criticisms cease to confront the science and the reality on which it is based, and seek to impose beliefs on reality. This is my definition of *ideology*: fixed beliefs about a changing reality. In this way it differs from science, which is testable and adaptable in its views of reality. Many of the attacks on climate science are ideological, not scientific.

In a previous section, we took a look at the "hockey stick," a graph that first appeared in the IPCC Third Assessment Report.[73] It is named for the shape of the curve that shows temperatures at a moderate level until the 20th century, when they begin to rise rapidly. It has been the subject of many attacks, particularly regarding the methodology of using proxies for estimating temperatures for the years before instruments such as thermometers were available. Among the most severe critiques is a book by Montford titled *Hockey Stick Illusion*,[74] which uses complex and contorted statistical techniques to try to reanalyze "hockey stick" research. Montford's work is based on critiques developed by Ross McKitrick and Stephen McIntyre, two statisticians with ties to fossil fuel industries. They have been characterized by one author as "quacks."[75] Using such statistical techniques to attack data presented by scientists is considered "alchemy" by another observer.[76] It is typical of denial ideologues who find it difficult to refute the science, so they resort to dubious methodologies.

IPCC reports and James Hansen's work, discussed above, have attracted severe criticism. One of the harshest critiques is from Patrick Michaels, a guru of denial ideology. He claims that Hansen used a model that predicted that temperatures would rise 0.45°C between 1988, when

Hansen testified before a Senate committee, and 1997, when Michaels testified before another Senate committee. In fact, they rose by only 0.11°C, implying that Hansen's model was inaccurate.[77] In fact, Hansen had predicted exactly 0.11°C under a "business as usual" scenario. The higher number, 0.45°C, was the "high" scenario. Michaels made it appear that Hansen predicted an increase of .45°C when the increase was only one fourth as much. Hansen's response to Michaels suggested that Michaels was "treading close to scientific fraud."[78]

Scenarios seem to trouble denial ideologues. Their approach often has been that if scientists cannot present a single prediction of future temperatures, they must be in error. They find it difficult to accept that climate scientists have projected different outcomes of global warming based on different levels of emissions. Sometimes these scenarios depend on projection of different rates of economic growth, resource use, population trends, etc., but their primary purpose is to lay out possibilities, not make predictions. Denial advocates such as Michaels will choose one of the scenarios and then say, "See, the predictions don't work—the temperature has not gone up as much as predicted." This is a complete misreading of climate science. The science is about projecting trends from variable inputs, not about predicting exact outcomes.

A number of climate scientists have made policy recommendations, including reduction of fossil fuel use, development of alternative sources of energy, and conservation of energy. If the science is well established, why do public and opinion leaders' reactions to climate change policy prescriptions by scientists continue to be negative? The science itself does not contain specific prescriptions. Projections of climate changes, however, suggest conclusions about carbon emissions. These conclusions imply that energy use must change if the worst consequences of climate change are to be avoided. This approach requires policies that threaten some basic interests in our societies. In particular, these basic interests involve fossil fuel industries, whose role as the primary source of energy for economic growth and high living standards is paramount in modern societies. These interests are expressed through organizations that purport to have expertise in climate science, but whose credentials are often dubious.[79] The National Coal Association and the Edison Electric Institute are interest groups with significant influence on Congress. Denial movements mobilize contrarian scientists without regard to their credentials or connections with mainstream climate science. Denial movements use dubious scientific statements as "proof" that climate change is (1) not happening or (2) not dangerous enough to merit emissions limits. These arguments are presented as scientific findings, but the arguments are not peer reviewed.

A disjunction of science and journalism pervades the reporting on climate change.[80] News about climate is sometimes inaccurate at best, and misleading at worst. Journalists try to "balance" their reporting by looking for two sides in a purported "controversy." Denial ideologues who claim that scientists disagree about climate science mislead the journalists. The idea that there is a controversy in the climate science community is a red herring often used by contrarians because it implies that we do not need to worry about consequences of climate change when applying the findings to issues of economic growth and resource use.

Because the contrarians present alternative explanations and try to refute mainstream climate science, mass media writers and commentators present their pseudoscience as one side of a controversy with credible science as the other side. Since the contrarians have full confidence in their "findings" while mainstream scientists offer caveats to their findings with confidence limits, the contrarians sometimes win the battle.[81]

A result of this seesaw of climate pseudoscience and climate science is confusion. With two competing explanations, the public becomes indifferent and adopts a wait-and-see posture. "The confusion that bipolar framing has engendered creates in the public at large a sense that 'if the experts don't know the answers, how can I, a mere lay citizen, fathom this complex situation?' "[82]

Promoting controversy about climate science is a favorite tactic of groups such as the Cato Institute, partly funded by money from Koch Industries. One of Cato's lead scientists is Patrick Michaels, former climatologist for the state of Virginia. Michaels conducted a "survey" in which he claimed that most US scientists oppose the IPCC: "Visitors to the website of *Scientific American* have been invited to participate in an ongoing survey on global warming. This survey finds…that only a tiny minority (16%) agree that the IPCC is an effective group of government representatives, scientists, and other experts. Eighty-four percent agree, however, that it is a corrupt organization, prone to groupthink, with a political agenda."[83]

Use of statistics such as those cited by Michaels to criticize the IPCC is a common tactic by critics of climate science. The intended audience may not check the accuracy of these statistics, and in this case the statistics were wildly inaccurate. An editor of *Scientific American* responded to Michaels's testimony as follows: "The testimony of Patrick J. Michaels demonstrates the climate-skeptic strategy of systematically selecting portions of a number of actual scientific studies, not just this poll, to make an argument that is counter to the prevailing body of scientific evidence about climate change." She found the misuse of these studies offensive: "I personally deplore such misrepresentations of science and was dismayed to see *Scientific American*'s good name put to that purpose."[84]

Patrick Michaels's organization, Cato Institute has influenced the climate debate. Public acceptance of climate science has weakened under the assault of climate contrarians. This is a tactic used by other industries affected by scientific findings, such as the tobacco industry, which resisted findings used by the surgeon general in the 1960s to link smoking and cancer.

Koch Industries and the Koch Foundations have used pseudoscience to influence public opinion, with some degree of success. The decline in the number of Americans who believe that global warming is caused by human activities is due in part to the portrayal of climate science as "controversial," even though a vast majority of scientists disagree.[85]

When skeptics and denial proponents plan political strategy, they apply the principle of "uncertainty" in crafting their messages. This exploits the confusion and misunderstanding of science that is inherent in the public view of research and their confidence in results. Scientists always include uncertainty or probability estimates in their findings, but denial ideologues will use this standard practice to suggest that there are controversies in climate science. Any controversy is treated as a clash of equally valid approaches and becomes the basis for claiming lack of certainty as justification for business as usual. In a 2002 memo, the Republican political consultant Frank Luntz wrote that no action is required so long as "voters believe there is no consensus about global warming within the scientific community."[86] Contrarians who try to convince politicians and opinion leaders that the science is not sound often drive these reactions.

One of the leading voices of denial ideology is Fox News, part of Rupert Murdoch's News International empire. Fox News continues to report dubious information as science and distorts the work of scientists who have reported elsewhere. Fox seized on a report on temperature records in the Antarctic to "prove" that the Medieval Warming Period was as warm as today's global temperatures.[87] Fox has attempted to use this research to support the denial argument that the Medieval Warming Period extended across the globe. This argument is used to attack the findings that global temperatures are rising more today than in the past 1,000 years. Unfortunately for Fox News, the geochemist cited in the article, Zunli Lu, disagreed with their conclusions. "It is unfortunate that my research...has been misrepresented by a number of media outlets."[88] Although scientists can sometimes refute the errors that have been introduced into the interpretation of their work, the corrections do not always catch up to the misinformation. In this case, Fox printed the "news" a week after the refutation, ignoring Dr. Lu's correction.

Other denial ideologues have used the Medieval Warming Period, also called the Medieval Optimum, to criticize the "hockey stick" graph that allegedly minimizes this earlier warm period. While there is evidence that the Medieval Optimum was warm, this does not refute the analysis of human-induced warming at present.[89] In other words, the attempt by denial ideologues to explain both the Medieval Warming Period and the current warming as results of solar influences on earth's climate do not hold up. Denial attempts to refute climate science as invalid because of the equally high temperatures during the Medieval Warming Period and today are also specious.

Contrarians tend to reject climate models as inventions of climate scientists, with no basis in reality. They are playing on laymen's belief that the only thing that can prove a theory is observations. The problem with relying solely on observations is that they do not show the consequences of observed trends. When climate scientists use temperature and GHG emissions data from the past to project future temperatures, they are using observations but going beyond the present to project changes in the future. This often leaves them open to questioning by critics, but the projections are solidly based on analysis of past and current data.

An example of the misuse of climate models to support denial ideology is from a book by Ralph B. Alexander titled *Global Warming False Alarm*. He quotes the 2007 IPCC report that says "anthropogenic climate change must be pursued by demonstrating that the detected change is consistent with computer model simulations." He then goes on to criticize IPCC by restating this: "Must be pursued by computer simulations? In a single sweeping declaration, the IPCC brushes aside modern science."[90] This misstatement leaves out the key words "demonstrating that the detected change is consistent with computer model simulations." IPCC models are not "pursued" but are confirmed by detected changes in the data.

Another tendency of critics is to focus on the scientists rather than the science. Scientists are particularly vulnerable to attacks when they make statements or proposals that threaten established beliefs or ways of living.[91] Critics capitalize on this vulnerability by attacking climate scientists. They do so by *ad hominem* attacks that accuse researchers of cynically promoting research projects by using alarmist tactics. In other words, the climate scientists are portrayed as cynical manipulators who use climate projections to scare governments into funding their research, and who act as gatekeepers to control what is published.[92]

A more derisive form of *ad hominem* attacks simply asserts that climate scientists are greedy and lazy, as exemplified by this example from Rush Limbaugh: "The overwhelming body of science has been bought! The overwhelming body of science has been purchased...It's much easier to siphon off grants and people are willing to pay you for a belief. They're willing to reward you for producing a paper, even if it is based in junk science and a hoax."[93] Limbaugh uses two of the most common themes in denial ideology: "junk science" and "siphoning off grants." He accuses scientists of manipulating or fabricating data in order to obtain funding.

Critics often exploit the lay view that changes in the weather are not significant and therefore not evidence of climate change. They also claim that temperature changes may even benefit some. Glenn Beck has described global warming as a good thing because it may make the Northeast United States more pleasant. "I would like approximately 30 degrees of global warming in the winter, followed by a 10-degree global cooling in the summer. A gentle global breeze would be nice too."[94] To some extent, this view of climate change is facetious, as befits a self-described "rodeo clown." Glenn Beck does more than raise specious claims about how uncertainty and bias undermine climate science, however. He accuses scientists and proponents of climate policies of persecuting climate skeptics. In one broadcast, "Climate of Fear," he compared climate science to the Holocaust.[95]

Beck's reference to Nazism is not accidental. There is a conspiracy theory circulating in the denialsphere that attributes climate science to a Nazi: "One of the primary pioneering theorists on apocalyptic global warming is Guenther Schwab (1902–2006), an Austrian Nazi."[96] The Nazi affiliation of one scientist is expanded to include the environmental movement: "Long before Al Gore's *Inconvenient Truth*, green Nazi Guenther Schwab played a large role in catalyzing the frightening theory of global warming. With no small thanks to Schwab, the Great Tribulation of Global Warming was ushered into the modern consciousness behind the collapse of the Millennial 1,000-year Third Reich."[97]

This weird juxtaposition of the "Great Tribulation of Global Warming" with the Third Reich is an extreme example of critics accusing scientists of evil motives or ideologies. To some extent, this is a common rhetorical device; many ideologues are fond of using Nazism as an analogy for evil. Sen. James Inhofe (R-OK) uses a similar analogy: "It kind of reminds...I could use the Third Reich, the big lie. You say something over and over and over and over again, and people will believe it, and that's their strategy."[98]

While this kind of criticism is rather extreme, it is not unfamiliar in denial ideology. A number of other attacks on climate science attribute evil to the scientists or accuse them of nefarious activities. Attacks on the scientists are often used to avoid confronting the "hard" facts of the science itself, facts that cannot be easily refuted by the critics.

Many contrarians rely on arguments that scientists use alarmism to solicit research funding. These attacks escalated in 2009 when a hacker obtained and publicized e-mails from the Climatic Research Unit (CRU) at East Anglia University in the United Kingdom. While the e-mails, often called "Climategate," showed poor judgment on the part of the researchers, they did not disprove the scientific findings of the unit or other scientists. Nevertheless, the researchers became objects of attack on a personal level. Purportedly the e-mails show that the scientists are greedy and unscrupulous. Most of the attacks are on the scientists rather than the science. Four different investigations have cleared the CRU of the charge of fabricating data. Nevertheless, contrarians continue to use the e-mails to try to demonstrate that the science is not valid.[99]

Because climate scientists are bearers of bad news, they become unpopular. The American Academy for the Advancement of Science (AAAS, one of the leading science organizations in the world) has lamented the effect this has on the scientists:

> We are deeply concerned by the extent and nature of personal attacks on climate scientists. Reports of harassment, death threats, and legal challenges have created a hostile environment that inhibits the free exchange of scientific findings and ideas and makes it

difficult for factual information and scientific analyses to reach policymakers and the public. This both impedes the progress of science and interferes with the application of science to the solution of global problems. AAAS vigorously opposes attacks on researchers that question their personal and professional integrity or threaten their safety based on displeasure with their scientific conclusions.[100]

Sometimes the critics go beyond attacks on climate scientists and attack the facts. The apparent purpose is to plant misinformation in the mind of the public and thus to undermine the credibility of climate science. In a blatant example of misinformation, the newsletter *Human Events* published an article claiming that the warmest period on record was 70 years ago: "Since [the 1800s] the temperature on the planet has only warmed 0.7°C (or slightly more than a degree Fahrenheit), with most of that warming occurring before 1940. In fact, according to the National Climatic Data Center, the warmest decade on record was the 1930s...the hottest year on record was 1934."[101]

This canard about warming in the past has been echoing around the denialsphere, and many pick it up.[102] It has been refuted, however, by scientists, including James Hansen and NOAA. Hansen stated in 2005: "It is no longer correct to say that 'most global warming occurred before 1940.' More accurately, there was slow global warming, with large fluctuations, over the century up to 1975, and subsequent rapid warming of almost 0.2°C [0.4°F] per decade."[103]

The canard makes reference to NOAA's National Climatic Data Center in the article, but this is what the NOAA website states about temperature in the past century: "The decadal global land and ocean average temperature anomaly for 2001–2010 was the warmest decade on record for the globe, with a surface global temperature of 0.56°C (1.01°F) above the 20th-century average. This surpassed the previous decadal record (1991–2000) value of 0.36°C (0.65°F). The 2010 Northern Hemisphere combined global land and ocean surface temperature was the warmest year on record, at 0.73°C (1.31°F) above the 20th-century average."[104]

Why would *Human Events* publish misinformation so easily refuted with fact checking? Perhaps it is because they think that readers are convinced by the denial argument that government scientists are charlatans or worse, or that readers would not check the facts. Readers of *Human Events* are likely to be followers of the denial movement. In any case, the facts refute the assertion that the warmest decade was the 1930s and the warmest year was 1934.

A common argument critics use is that increases in CO_2 levels follow increases in temperatures, and that warming is just a natural phenomenon that comes and goes. This argument is used to try to refute the findings in climate science that anthropogenic CO_2 emissions are a cause of global warming. One critic made the following statement with no documentation: "There doesn't appear to be much, if any, correlation between CO_2 contributions from human activities and temperature fluctuations."[105]

This assertion, like many critics use, is stated flatly with little or no explanation or reference to research. It completely contradicts the solid body of climate research (NRC, 2010) that shows causation between CO_2 increases and temperature increases. "Climate contrarians have argued that because temperature has an effect on CO_2, there is no need for CO_2 to drive temperature. This is a silly argument; there is no reason why the cause-and-effect relationship between CO_2 and temperature cannot be a two-way street."[106]

Denial assertions that increases in CO_2 follow, rather than precede, temperature rises are canards that appear throughout the ideology. Because historic and geological data do show that CO_2 increases sometimes follow temperature increases, denial advocates generalize and assert that CO_2 increases always follow temperature increases and therefore cannot be blamed for global warming. This assertion has been refuted by experimental research as well as atmospheric measurements. About 7% of temperature increases occurred before the CO_2 rise, whereas 93% of global warming followed the CO_2 increase.[107]

The IPCC has had so much influence on climate science that it has spawned a "Nongovernmental IPCC" (NIPCC) to refute the IPCC Fourth Assessment Report.[108] The NIPCC screed, from the Center for the Study of Carbon Dioxide and Global Change (CSCDGC), is co-authored by Fred Singer, published by Heartland Institute (an AstroTurf organization; see chapter 2), and supported by coal and oil industry money. The NIPCC makes its case with a number of criticisms of the IPCC work based on attacks on models used for IPCC reports.[109] When the IPCC released its 2013 report, the NIPCC countered with a report that claimed, "Doubling the concentration of atmospheric CO_2 from its preindustrial level, in the absence of other forcings and feedbacks, would likely cause a warming of ~0.3 to 1.1°C, almost 50% of which must already have occurred. A few tenths of a degree of additional warming, should it occur, would not represent a climate crisis."[110] In other words, the NIPCC downplayed the "climate sensitivity" of CO_2 increases, claiming that rising greenhouse gases would have little effect. Most climate scientists have refuted this claim.[111]

Singer and associates attack the very core of the IPCC process, projections based on modeling. They use the arguments of "invalid scientific procedures," "opinions of scientists," a failure to "accurately simulate the physics of earth's radiative energy balance," and "major model imperfections." Climate scientists, whose models have been verified by temperature measurements and other data, have refuted these criticisms.[112] Models do have uncertainties, but these do not invalidate them. "The amount of uncertainty in such projections can be estimated to some extent by comparing forecasts made by many different models, with their different parameterizations."[113]

A source of misunderstanding of models is the denial claim that all climate scientists are using the same model or very similar models. This is completely untrue. Different groups, with dissimilar models, various sources of funding, and different biases, have come to the same conclusions.[114] So much for the denial claim that climate science is a conspiracy of like-minded fraudsters. Models may not all agree on everything or have the same specific findings, but they do agree on the general trend of global warming. Models are not perfect; none will predict with absolute accuracy the temperature or climate in years to come. But all of them point in the same direction: increasing global average temperatures.[115] Models may be "wrong" in the sense that they do not precisely predict weather for a given day fifty years hence, but they are necessary to analyze the trends of climate change.

While criticizing climate science, NIPCC uses the "scientific method" in an egregious manner. It "mines the scientific literature for nuggets of contrary evidence and doubt" and "ignores mountains of evidence about the adverse effects of global warming."[116] Although its effects on the science are negligible, NIPCC and the Center for the Study of Carbon Dioxide and Global Change (CSCDGC) have more forceful effects on the politics of climate change. CSCDGC sent a letter to Congress signed by a number of scientists to claim that the "mainstream" science is wrong based on "678 scientific studies."

> Do the 678 scientific studies…cited in the NIPCC report, provide real-world evidence (as opposed to theoretical climate model predictions) for global warming-induced increases in the worldwide number and severity of floods? **No**. In the global number and severity of droughts? **No**. In the number and severity of hurricanes and other storms? **No**. Do they provide any real-world evidence of Earth's seas inundating coastal lowlands around the globe? **No**. Increased human mortality? **No**. Plant and animal extinctions? **No**. Declining vegetative productivity? **No**. More frequent and deadly coral bleaching? **No**. Marine life dissolving away in acidified oceans? **No**.[117]

This analysis attempts to invalidate basic climate science with a list of purported consequences of climate change attributed to scientists. It is difficult to link specific weather events to climate change,[118] but scientists have connected sea level rise, flooding, droughts, and intensity of storms to global warming.[119] As we have seen, there is evidence of declining "vegetative productivity" in agriculture[120] and sea level rise.[121] More indirectly, of course, the increases in mortality and extinction are projections from the likely consequences of drought, flooding, and hotter temperatures. Many of these consequences are projected on the basis of long-term trends. For example, scientists project sea level rise over several centuries, and the fact that levels have not risen much so far does not invalidate the projection. A brief, succinct, and brutal assessment of the NIPCC analysis in the report was made by scientists at Stanford University and Princeton. They dismissed it as "fabricated nonsense."[122]

The NIPCC critiques embody a host of denial canards. Among the most frequent misstatements in denial ideology is that "the average global temperature hasn't increased at all over the past decade," a statement that has been disproved by NOAA data cited earlier as well as IPCC reports. Another is that science treats CO_2 as "a poison," a misreading of the climate science view that CO_2 is a pollutant, not a poison. Scientists regard the different gases as separate chemicals with different effects. Concluding that the "CO_2 scare is a fraud" is an extension of the misreading of climate science to the point of accusing scientists of fraud.

Climate science is subject to review and revision just as much as any other field of science. When *Science* published an article suggesting revision of "climate sensitivity" projections, that is, the amount of warming expected from given levels of greenhouse gas emissions, critics seized on the report to indict all of climate science. The denial ideologues treated the article as a complete refutation of climate science, while all it suggested was a slight revision of the models. In spite of this modest proposal, critics used it to accuse climate scientists of "scientific fraud" and contended that the "warmist ideology is crumbling."[123]

Perhaps the most extreme critical statement is in a manifesto entitled "Energy and Climate Wars." In this manifesto, "AGW-ism" refers to climate science; it is an extension of the acronym for anthropogenic global warming. "As cyclical warming and cooling periods have always been the norm throughout history, one has to wonder why they insist that the usual parameters of natural temperature variation could not possibly apply today."[124] This assertion repeats the denial argument that climate change is natural, not man made. They go on to argue, "What it all boils down to is that the twin 'infallible' tenets or unassailable doctrines of AGW-ism are: 1) that its chief priests understand the science of climate when they clearly don't (it's too complicated with many factors, no one does), and 2) that carbon dioxide is the 'Great Satan' that must be defeated—when it plainly isn't (and there is, literally, zero empirical evidence for it)."[125]

In this critical vein, the identification of climate science as religion and scientists as priests is ironic. Many of the critics promote ideologies identified with particular religions, as we will see in chapters 2 and 4. Scientists would bridle at any suggestions that they have religious motives. Beliefs can indeed have irrational bases in religion, but the notion that climate science is a belief system is highly objectionable to most scientists.

One of the most egregious critical pieces written about climate science is Michael Crichton's *State of Fear.* As a novel, it avoids proof of accuracy in reporting scientific findings, but its premise is that environmentalists have formed a conspiracy to promote invalid versions of climate science. In posing the issues this way, the novel seems to convey some "truths" about climate science, but in fact it conveys only denial. An example is the "urban heat island effect," a presumably devastating critique of temperature measurements by climate scientists. Crichton misrepresented Jim Hansen's "prediction," described above as a set of scenarios presented during his 1988 testimony to Congress. Crichton claims that Hansen's data is inaccurate because of the "heat island effect." As Bowen notes, the false claim of "heat island effect" persists among denial ideologues.[126] As the Berkeley Earth Surface Temperature (BEST) research shows, the temperature findings of many climate scientists have corrected for the "heat island effect" and have been replicated numerous times.

"Heat island" canards came up when Anthony Watts tried to refute Muller's BEST research on the *PBS NewsHour* by citing the "heat island effect." This elicited a response from NOAA: "The American public can be confident in NOAA's long-standing surface temperature record, one of the world's most comprehensive, accurate, and trusted data sets."[127] The validity of the data enables scientists to argue that denial assertions about the "heat island effect" are irrelevant. "There is no doubt that NOAA's temperature record is scientifically sound and reliable. To ensure accuracy of the record, scientists use peer-reviewed methods to account for all potential inaccuracies in the temperature readings, such as changes in station location, instrumentation and replacement, and urban heat effects."[128] In this response, NOAA refuted two denial arguments: that the earth is cooling, and that climate science measurements are inaccurate.

In conclusion, criticism of climate science usually takes one of two forms: attacking the scientists using *ad hominem* arguments, such as greed or publicity seeking; or spreading misinformation about the science, such as solar cycles or past warming. (Solar cycles account for only 5% to 10% of global warming.) These are combined in *Climate of Corruption*,[129] which invokes "Climategate," local weather events, and anecdotal reports of a miscellany of climate misinformation to refute climate science. It amounts to a highly selective and sparsely documented collection of misinformation. This approach exemplifies the contrarian methodology of questioning climate science, supplying the denial movement's ideology and diverting public attention from scientifically sound global data and projections of global warming.

Chapter 2.
Denial Movements: Tea Party, AFP, Heartland Institute, and Cornwall Alliance

Climate change will have significant social implications, but there appears to be little preparation for the social changes that will occur. Societies will have to rebuild infrastructure, accommodate climate refugees (both from coastal areas of their own countries and from abroad), and redirect agricultural production. All of these changes will create tensions and problems because of the economic and social costs involved. Fear of these problems and exploitation of these tensions have given rise to social movements espousing a denial ideology.

At the core of the denial reactions is a psychological mechanism that has been studied in the context of other social movements.[130] Denial is a means of resolving what Leon Festinger and associates called "cognitive dissonance," the contradiction between what one believes and what one observes in reality.[131] Further, many social movements define themselves in opposition to the prevailing myths and beliefs of elites.[132] In other words, social movements have a vested interest in denying the prevailing views of reality and positing alternative views.

Beyond the psychological concept of dissonance, there are social conceptions that help explain the tenacity of denial. Another tendency of social movements that applies to denial of climate science is the collective nature of beliefs. "In sharp contrast to psychological approaches to denial, the notion of socially organized denial emphasizes that ignoring occurs in response to social circumstances and is carried out through a process of social interaction."[133] In other words, denial is not only a matter of personal disbelief; tendencies toward denial will be reinforced by membership in organizations that support denial. Denial is "socially organized," and individuals will resist information such as climate science because of social norms and interactions.[134]

When presented with information on climate science, people who are predisposed toward denial will maintain their position because it conforms to social norms and is nourished by interactions with others who deny climate science. This approach confirms the analysis of denial as an ideology, an interactive belief system that relies on the reinforcement of denial movements. Because of human psychology, it becomes difficult to overcome denial based on "willful ignorance and self-interest."[135] Dissonance is reinforced by denial because willful ignorance depends on justification through denial mechanisms. Only when we can find a rationale for not facing the facts of climate change can denial be sustained.

Consideration of the group context of denial ideology is confirmed by survey research, which indicates that information by itself has little effect. Social movements and political elites package information in a way that influences thinking about climate change. Climate science "advocacy" has "only a minor effect on public concern," but "political mobilization by elites and advocacy groups is critical in influencing climate change concern."[136] The principal significance of survey findings is that interpretation of climate science is shaped by the ideology of the elites and advocacy groups. By itself, science has "only a minor effect on public concern."[137]

With regard to terminology, the term *denial* may be contentious to some, but it is used here in only a descriptive manner with reference to climate science. Members of the denial movement complain that *denial* or *denier* is a loaded term associated with people who deny the Holocaust,[138] but that is not the purpose of its use here. It is simply the description of those who deny that climate change is caused by human activities, particularly the use of fossil fuels, or that the climate is changing at all. Any suggestion that it is associated with the Holocaust is a rhetorical device with no relevance to the analysis here.

Denial ideology is a leading example of the ideology of movements that tend to express ideas counter to prevailing ideas of societies and elites.[139] In the case of denial movements, the ideology has concepts and "facts" contradictory to climate science, which is viewed as an elitist ideology. Some denial advocates have even referred to climate science as *climatism*, as if it were only a belief system.[140] In fact, climate science is not made up of fixed beliefs about reality. Climate science findings change as research develops more information that either confirms or refutes hypotheses.

We will examine several different types of denial movements. Denial movements such as the Tea Party may have a populist tinge, but special interest groups have supported them. Most other groups tend to be "AstroTurf" organizations that exploit popular fears about the implications of climate science. In this context, *AstroTurf* refers to the fact that the movements pose as grassroots organizations but in fact are funded by special interests.

Tea Party

The most prominent denial movement in the United States of America is the Tea Party movement. While many of the denial groups (see below for Americans for Prosperity and Cornwall Alliance) are "AstroTurf" organizations with wealthy backers seeking to generate grassroots support, Tea Party groups are really populist groups. Their influence on Congress was evident in the 2013 government shutdown and debt-ceiling fracas. They are also having major effects on climate policies.

The Tea Party's "New Contract with America" proposes to "reject cap and trade" and "stop costly new regulations that would increase unemployment, raise consumer prices, and weaken the nation's global competitiveness with virtually no impact on global temperatures."[141] As is the case with many denial movements, the Tea Party questions climate science and claims that climate change is just an expression of natural cycles. One Tea Party leader said, "This so-called climate science is just ridiculous. I think it's all cyclical. Carbon regulation, cap and trade, it's all just a money-control avenue."[142]

Denial of climate change is not confined to just leaders of the Tea Party or politicians pandering to them. Most self-identified Tea Party followers deny climate science, while large majorities of Democrats and independents endorse it. Even a majority of Republicans other than the Tea Party followers endorse climate science.[143] Members of Congress elected with Tea Party support do not represent these Republicans (see chapter 4).

Tea Party members' denial of climate change is not based on ignorance, at least as far as survey respondents are concerned. They are much more likely than other groups to say they are "very well informed."[144] When asked which statement is closer to their views, Tea Party members were much more likely than other groups to say "there is a lot of disagreement among scientists about whether or not global warming is happening,"[145] a spurious claim based on statements by critics of climate science (chapter 1, above). A few, amounting to 13% of Tea Party supporters, believe that "most scientists think global warming is not happening," obtaining all their information on climate change from a tiny minority of contrarians. Tea Party ideologues sometimes cite contrarian scientists' work to make their point. But "the relative climate expertise and scientific prominence of [those contrarian] researchers…are substantially below that of the convinced researchers."[146]

One area where Tea Party members have a particular concern is education. They worry about the teaching of climate science as a kind of "secular religion." They sometimes complain that teachers convert children to this religion, which they call environmentalism, and question the authenticity of climate science.[147]

As we will see in the next section on the Heartland Institute, and in the section on state politics (chapter 4), denial ideology has a significant effect on education policies. Here the effect of Tea Party denial can be seen as an expression of "religious" conflict. Some, but not all, members of the Tea Party are religious conservatives who see science as an enemy. This view leads them to deny climate change on general principles, rather than to examine the validity of climate science itself. Sometimes the denial of climate science is paired with a denial of evolution. Both are involved in education policies.

One of the more organized segments of the Tea Party movement, the Tea Party Patriots, has produced a manifesto by two of its founders. In the discussion of federal agencies that "overreach" their power, the authors assert, "Despite Congress clearly rejecting the idea, the Environmental Protection Agency is trying to foist President Obama's cap-and-trade carbon tax on the American People."[148] This statement contains two common denial canards: that the Environmental Protection Agency is "foisting" a cap-and-trade system on the country, and that it is a tax. EPA regulations on carbon emissions are neither a cap-and-trade system nor a tax.

Local Tea Party organizations sometimes sponsor lectures by speakers who take rather extreme positions. An example is Donna Holt, executive director of the Virginia Campaign for Liberty, who blamed the "globalist totalitarian dictatorship" of climate science for imposing climate policies on America.[149] Using environmentalism as a ruse for "globalist totalitarian dictatorship" is a familiar theme in denial ideology. It harks back to the extreme conservatism of the 1950s and 1960s when the John Birch Society and other groups railed against the United Nations.[150] Most denial advocates do not go this far in openly speaking about conspiracies. Sen. James Inhofe (R-OK), for example, condemns climate science "internationalism" as "antisovereignty" because it imposes limits on national policies.[151]

Tea Party local leaders can also be involved in other antienvironmental causes. Most stakeholders, including environmentalists, businesses, tribes, and fishermen, approved the Klamath River Basin Restoration Agreement in Southern Oregon and Northern California in 2010. When that happened, a group of farmers and a machine-shop owner formed a local Tea Party and stopped the project.[152] Although the agreement would have restored salmon habitat and had support from most of the area's residents and businesses, Tea Party followers blocked it. The role of the Tea Party is like that of many pressure groups: by focusing the strength of a minority of stakeholders, it can stop programs that have a support of the majority. Another favorite target of Tea Party activists is the United Nations, which they blame for everything, including local problems. Local efforts to control sprawl and conserve energy through public transportation and preservation of open space have drawn the ire of some Tea Party activists.[153]

It might be said that environmentalists advocate controlling sprawl and conserving energy as part of their efforts to reduce greenhouse gas emissions, but it can hardly be said that the United Nations is part of a "conspiracy to deny property rights and herd citizens toward cities." The United Nations Framework Convention on Climate Change (UNFCCC) does not try to negotiate such specific policies for member states. There are guidelines for land use planning in Agenda 21, the UN document negotiated in Rio during the 1992 UN Conference on Environment and Development (UNCED), the "Rio Summit." Labeling these guidelines as a "UN-led conspiracy" is a favorite tactic of the denial movement. These charges led Arizona to consider legislation to outlaw Agenda 21 principles. Other states are considering similar legislation and resolutions.[154]

All of these bills and resolutions raise the question, why is Agenda 21 so threatening to state legislators? To most observers, Agenda 21 is a rather innocuous set of environmental principles such as the "precautionary principle." In denial ideology, fear plays a major role. Fear of the "black helicopters," mythical UN enforcers and other outside forces, overrides any consideration of the principles embodied in Agenda 21. The association of Agenda 21 with negotiation of UNFCCC, both of which were approved at the Rio Earth Summit in 1992, means that climate change negotiations are tarred with the same brush.

One of the ideological tenets of the denial movement is that "man has dominion over the earth" and that "nature should serve man, not the other way around." Members of the Tea Party have blamed environmentalism for reversing the priorities of man and nature. The Tea Party-affiliated Virginia Campaign for Liberty claims, "Environmentalists have always had an agenda to put nature above man."[155]

Members of the Tea Party who are also Christian evangelists may subscribe to these views more than other members, who are not as inclined to mix politics and religion. Tea Party members are not all Christian evangelists, and the movement generally has avoided religion and politics. There is a movement that is much more willing to mix the two, however: the Cornwall Alliance.

Cornwall Alliance

The Cornwall Alliance, a Christian group affiliated with Roy Spencer and supported by Koch Industries, portrays itself as an alternative to other evangelical groups that have concerns about climate change. It produces newsletters and a video, *Resisting the Green Dragon*, a metaphor for environmentalism. Ironically, as a religious movement, the Cornwall Alliance attributes an occult religious motivation to climate scientists. The argument draws on a historic analogy to cargo cults, South Pacific religious groups that originated in the 1940s. It suggests that "scientists and politicians use this environmentalist Cargo Cult Science to make the most incredible predictions of future doom."[156] It is ironic that the Cornwall Alliance would attribute religious motives to climate scientists when some observers would say that unfettered growth is a religion. Perhaps it intends to use religion only as a metaphor for scientists' purported ideological tendencies.[157] But ideology cuts both ways. One analyst compares "growth fetishism" to the cargo cult religion.[158] Believers seem to think that growth is "conjured from thin air."

The Cornwall Alliance itself is an example of movements that use religion as a basis of ideology—for example, the "biblical viewpoint on environmental issues." The Cornwall Alliance asserts that environmentalists make nature a priority in "green policy," and this contradicts biblical beliefs. It invokes the biblical doctrines of the "Fall" and "Curse," presumably referring to man's expulsion from the Garden of Eden, "according to which nothing in nature is 'normal.' "[159] The Cornwall Alliance criticizes the "pantheism and biological egalitarianism of so much of the environmental movement."[160] It uses the term "biological egalitarianism" as a straw man for environmental concepts such as protection of nature, biodiversity, or climate stability.

The movement implies that human dominion over nature is a higher value and that environmentalism is anti-Christian.

As a denial movement, the Cornwall Alliance uses the denial argument that addressing climate change will lower living standards. This is a standard denial tactic, playing on the fears of people who worry about limits on their use of energy. In the case of the Cornwall Alliance, this is embellished by calling on Christians to fight the "environmentalism religion." "You, as an individual, have a tremendously important role to play in the church's battle against this impostor, with its alternative world view, its substitute doctrines of God, creation, man sin, and salvation, and its lethal mix of bogus science." The Cornwall Alliance then goes on to assert that climate science is based on "Marxist economics that threaten to fulfill the radical environmentalists' and deep ecologists' dream of ending industrial society and forcing humanity back into a primitive lifestyle—in which, as Thomas Hobbes put it, life was solitary, poor, nasty, brutish, and short."[161] Quoting Hobbes to reinforce fear of climate science is a special touch—with the usual mix of "bogus science" and "Marxist economics" reinforced by a philosophic cliché.

The Cornwall Alliance has produced a "declaration" to express denial ideology and has requested that followers sign it to indicate their opposition to climate science. It contains several misstatements: global warming is natural, there is no evidence of human contribution, CO2 is not a pollutant, reducing greenhouse gases will not reduce future global temperatures, and benefits would not exceed costs of mitigation.[162] Why are these statements misstatements? Let's take them one by one.

The first two repeat the denial argument that global warming is natural and there is "no convincing scientific evidence" that humans contribute to global warming. This has been disproved through a number of IPCC reports and scientific studies that verify the IPCC findings.[163]

The statement "We deny that carbon dioxide—essential to all plant growth—is a pollutant"[164] misrepresents both fact and law. Carbon dioxide is a pollutant in sufficient concentrations—such as those that killed 1,700 residents near Lake Nyos in Cameroon—but the more important fact is that carbon dioxide becomes increasingly dangerous worldwide as concentrations rise from 270 parts per million (ppm) in preindustrial air to 400 ppm today. In law, carbon dioxide is considered a pollutant under the Clean Air Act, which explicitly mentions climate, a finding that was confirmed by the Supreme Court.

The last argument, "Reducing greenhouse gases cannot achieve significant reductions in future global temperatures, and the costs of the policies would far exceed the benefits,"[165] denies the basic science of atmospheric chemistry. Scientists from Tyndall on have established the direct relationship between greenhouse gases and temperature. Economists including Nicholas Stern and William Nordhaus have established that the costs of policies would be much smaller than the benefits, depending on how soon those policies start.

The Cornwall Alliance also weighs in on the jobs-energy argument and belittles the effect of carbon dioxide. It argues that the EPA's climate regulations rest on a "false premise that Earth's climate system is extremely fragile," and that a "minute change" of CO2 concentrations from "27 thousandths of 1% to 39 thousandths of 1%" would not affect the climate. It criticizes the "moral case" of other evangelicals.[166]

The "moral case" to which the Cornwall Alliance refers is made by a group of religious organizations, including the National Religious Partnership for the Environment, Interfaith Power and Light, and the American Values Network. They are the objects of the Cornwall Alliance's wrath because they advocate GHG regulation and other climate actions. The Cornwall Alliance has stated its belief in the resilience of the climate system by saying that it is "robust, resilient, self-regulating, and self-correcting, admirably suited for human flourishing, and displaying His glory."[167] It also misstates that climate science is based on a false premise that "minute changes" in the atmosphere have major effects. It is precisely these "minute changes" that drive climate change.

Some evangelical Christians have responded in kind. Speaking of the principal writer of the Cornwall Alliance Newsletter, Calvin Beisner, and his ally Rush Limbaugh, the Christian Post says: "Beisner and Limbaugh, in peddling the notion that God designed the earth and its atmosphere to be immune from mankind's actions, are also implying that we can do anything we want to it without serious consequence."[168] The concept of "immunity" from mankind's actions is an important corollary to the idea that "man has dominion over the earth," which enables denial ideologues to ignore the effect of human-induced greenhouse gas emissions.

In chapters 3 and 4, the Cornwall Alliance's statements on ethics and politics will be examined in the context of culture and politicians' beliefs.

Heartland Institute

The Heartland Institute can be viewed as an "AstroTurf" movement linked with vested interests such as energy companies and their well-oiled think tanks. It tends to use two basic arguments: (1) scientific uncertainty, fraud, and special interests of climate scientists undermine the validity of global warming projections, and (?) any policy to reduce emissions would increase costs, taxes, and government spending. These are standard arguments of the fossil fuel industry when it seeks to deflect restrictions on fossil fuel use. Heartland uses denial arguments such as "scientific fraud" and contends that climate policies would mean "utterly unnecessary and truly harmful limitations on human progress."[169] Here the phrase "human progress" is a code phrase for fossil-fueled growth, which would be limited by climate policies stemming from the "subjective opinion" of climate science. The Heartland Institute thus touches on two principal beliefs in denial ideology: (1) that the science is "subjective" and not valid, and (2) that the policies are limitations on progress. In addition, the institute repeats the canard that global temperatures are cooling, a canard that circulates around the denialsphere.

Heartland's president, Joe Bast, has indicated some frustration with the fact that Heartland's views are not universally adopted. "We've won the public opinion debate, and we've won the political debate as well…but the scientific debate is a source of enormous frustration."[170] It seems presumptive to say that the Heartland Institute has won the public opinion debate if one examines poll results reported in this book.

Most polls show that a majority of the US public agrees that there is anthropogenic climate change and that something needs to be done about it.[171] It is perhaps somewhat more arguable that the Heartland Institute has "won" the political debate, since many in Congress and some presidential candidates have adopted denial ideology. (See chapter 4.) What is most interesting about this statement, however, is the "enormous frustration" with the scientific debate. Perhaps the Heartland Institute has unwittingly indicated that it is on the losing side of any "scientific debate" because its position is untenable. It holds annual meetings featuring denial advocates, but they have not had any effect on climate science. Heartland's meetings are mostly about ideology, and scientists tend to avoid them.

Some participants in Heartland Institute meetings go even further and accuse climate science of being a "Trojan horse" for communism. "To what extent is this entire movement simply a green Trojan horse, whose belly is full with red Marxist socioeconomic doctrine?"[172] Heartland invokes the classical "red scare" to try to discredit climate science, a tactic that would seem to have little effect in the 21st century.

In the run-up to its 2012 annual conference, Heartland generated some controversy about a billboard featuring Unabomber Ted Kaczynski, saying "I still believe in global warming, do you?" When asked about this, James Taylor of Heartland said that "alarmists" (climate scientists) use the same tactics. He said that Heartland invited "alarmists" to Heartland conferences but that they declined.[173] This begs the question, how should climate scientists regard movements such as Heartland? Since these movements like to frame climate science as an "either-or" proposition with published climate scientists on one side and Heartland's hired gun scientists on the other, it would seem reasonable for them to avoid the organization. Denial movements like to "teach the controversy" (see below) and claim that their version of climate science has the same validity as internationally recognized valid climate science. Climate scientists dismiss this claim, however.

Many climate scientists find it unacceptable to participate in Heartland's conferences, which would legitimate its claims. Chances are good that Heartland will not be holding any more conferences. President Joseph Bast said, "I hope to see you at a future conference, but at this point we have no plans to do another ICCC [International Conference on Climate Change]." He was probably referring to a lack of funding for future conferences.[174] Many businesses have withdrawn support, and Heartland's prospects for more meetings are doubtful.

Use of the Unabomber billboard backfired when a number of corporate sponsors, including State Farm Insurance, USAA, Eli Lilly, PepsiCo, and General Motors, withdrew funding from Heartland. Heartland then attributed this loss of funding to the environmental movement and complained that it "has long been a prime target of the environmental left for committing the 'sin' of highlighting observable climate data that has proved inconvenient to the narrative of global warming alarmism."[175] It is more likely that the corporations that had previously funded Heartland conferences were finding them counterproductive and distasteful. Nevertheless, Heartland continues to maintain that the billboard campaign was effective.[176] It excuses its tactics by saying that Heartland acknowledges that not all climate scientists are criminals like Kaczynski.

It is generous of Heartland to acknowledge that "not all global warming alarmists are murderers or tyrants." But Heartland still considers them lawbreakers and uses "guilt by association" to tar them with the same brush as mass murderers. This is an example of an *ad hominem* argument gone wild—an indictment of climate scientists whose work Heartland goes to extremes to refute. By using such extreme language, Heartland lowers its participation in the dialogue to a lowbrow level. It is difficult to see how any dialogue can continue at this level. It is obvious why climate scientists have declined to participate in any Heartland conferences. Even some of the leading lights of climate denial are objecting. Ross McKitrick, one of the main critics of the "hockey stick" (chapter 1), withdrew from the conference and objected that Heartland has gone too far.[177]

The Heartland Institute does more than hold meetings. Its pronouncements on climate change influence state politics. Environmental policy fellow James Taylor noted that Heartland supports "teaching the controversy," the idea that schools should present "both sides" of the supposed climate debate. This is a common theme of denial ideology, which tries to promote denial as "one side" of a debate with climate science. In fact, it is not an alternative to climate science; it is ideology. Nevertheless, Taylor said that Heartland supported efforts by state legislatures to ensure that taxpayer dollars are not spent in a manner that turns an important and ongoing scientific debate into a propaganda assault on impressionable students."[178] Ironically, the only propaganda assault is Heartland's use of denial propaganda. "Teaching the controversy" is a standard denial tactic, and misinformation about "an important and ongoing scientific debate" is introduced into state legislatures and school systems. (See chapter 4.) Even though 97% of climate scientists agree on basic findings, denial advocates ignore this and try to introduce doubt through their tactics.

The Heartland Institute is involved in other efforts to "teach the controversy" about climate science. These efforts include payments for developing a curriculum for denial and doubt about climate science. It funded a proposal by Dr. David Wojick, labeled a "consultant" to the Department of Energy, to develop a curriculum based on a premise that climate science is controversial and uncertain. Heartland reportedly considers educators "heavily biased toward the alarmist perspective" and spent $100,000 to develop a curriculum of 20 modules denying climate science by denying students the opportunity to learn about climate change.

Wojick has been a consultant to DOE (the Department of Energy) but not an expert on climate. "David Wojick has been a part-time support contractor for the Office of Scientific and Technical Information since 2003, working to help the office manage and organize its electronic databases. He has never advised or conducted research for the Department on climate change or any other scientific topic, and the office he works for is not a research organization," according to DOE.[179] He is a "contributing editor" to *Environment & Climate News,* a publication of the Heartland Institute.

A controversy developed around leaks of e-mails that contained Heartland's education strategy. Apparently the education strategy paper is authentic: "One of Heartland's fund-raising documents lays out the group's plans to spend $100,000 per year to develop a curriculum for schools that would call basic climate science into question…A senior fellow at Heartland confirmed these general details."[180] James Taylor of Heartland said, "We are concerned that schools are teaching climate change issues in a manner that is not consistent with sound science and that is designed to lead students to the erroneous belief that humans are causing a global warming crisis." Heartland goes on to indicate its goal in the campaign: "**We hope that our efforts will restore sound science to climate change education** and discourage the political propaganda that too often passes as 'education.' "[181] "Sound science" is a buzzword for denial ideology; anything but deniers' view of the science is considered "junk science" unworthy of teaching.

The Heartland Institute itself publishes documents of dubious scientific value. One of these is a "report" by the Non-Governmental International Panel on Climate Change (NIPCC).[182] It purports to show that there is no human-induced climate change, and that the scientific models of the IPCC are invalid. However, most scientists regard its findings as invalid.

The Heartland Institute is not only concerned about keeping climate science out of schools; it wants to keep it out of the press as well. When *Forbes* magazine published reports from climate scientist Peter Gleick, Heartland reportedly responded that it wanted to keep "opposing voices" out of *Forbes*.[183] Gleick's work involves hydroclimatology, the study of the impact of climate change on ocean temperatures and water resources. He received a MacArthur Fellowship for his work. He has written articles for the press as well as peer-reviewed journals, and it is the press articles that got him into trouble with the Heartland Institute. He later admitted that he was the whistleblower who received Heartland documents, some of which he solicited through a fake e-mail address. Heartland threatened to take legal action, and Gleick's attorney John Keker said that Gleick would welcome the opportunity to go to court:

"Dr. Gleick looks forward to using discovery to understand more about the veracity of the documents, lay bare the implications of Heartland's propaganda plans, and, in particular, determine once and for all who is truly behind Heartland and why," Keker said.[184]

With regard to the ethics of leaking Heartland documents, a group of scientists who had been victimized by the Climategate leaks (see chapter 1) responded in "An Open Letter to the Heartland Institute":

> As scientists who have had their e-mails stolen, posted online, and grossly misrepresented, we can appreciate the difficulties the Heartland Institute is currently experiencing following the online posting of the organization's internal documents earlier this week… We know what it feels like to have private information stolen and posted online via illegal hacking. It happened to climate researchers in 2009 and again in 2011. Personal e-mails were culled through and taken out of context before they were posted online. In 2009, the Heartland Institute was among the groups that spread false allegations about what these stolen e-mails said.

Touché! The scientists go on to say:

> Despite multiple independent investigations, which demonstrated that allegations against scientists were false, the Heartland Institute continued to attack scientists based on the stolen e-mails. When more stolen e-mails were posted online in 2011, the Heartland Institute again pointed to their release and spread false claims about scientists. So although we can agree that stealing documents and posting them online is not an acceptable practice, we would be remiss if we did not point out that the Heartland Institute has had no qualms about utilizing and distorting e-mails stolen from scientists.[185]

"Heartlandgate" and Heartland's policies may lead to increasing polarization of the climate policy debate (see chapter 4). The immediate issue is the effect of denial ideology on education, but in the long run it will also affect public opinion and politics. Heartland is undermining, through its attacks on scientists, the public credibility of climate science and forestalling actions that might reduce the future consequences of climate change.

Some of the documents purloined from the Heartland Institute indicated that corporations such as General Motors have contributed to the organization. Although GM did not contribute directly to the program that allegedly supports teaching denial in the schools, it has contributed to other educational programs at Heartland. As a result, some opponents of denial ideology have circulated a petition to GM to stop the contributions. The petition was reportedly signed by 20,000 people and sent to GM.[186] While petitions do not always spur action, this seems to have had some influence on GM.[187] It has withdrawn funding from Heartland.

Michael Mann, author of the "hockey stick" (chapter 1), has said that Heartland tends to "attack climate science," and "manufacture false controversy."[188] Mann, like many other scientists, has been perplexed by the effect of Heartland propaganda. Has Heartland Institute had an effect on denial ideology? According to its own polls, it has been particularly effective with local and state officials. It claims that 79% of state legislators and 63% of local officials read Heartland publications, and that 45% of state legislatures say these publications led to a change in public policy.[189]

As we will see in chapter 4, the greatest impact seems to be at the state level, with many legislatures following the Heartland "party line" about climate science. This is usually expressed in the form of resolutions against EPA regulations or declarations that climate science is not valid and should not be used for policy decisions.

The Heartland Institute has formed alliances, and indeed has common funding, with other denial organizations, notably the American Legislative Exchange Council and Americans for Prosperity, both funded by Koch money.[190]

Americans for Prosperity

Among the tactics of denial movements is pressure on legislators at all levels of government to reject climate change legislation, using the rationale that policies such as cap and trade amount to "carbon taxes" and thus violate the principle of limited government and reduced taxation. Americans for Prosperity, an "AstroTurf" organization supported by Koch money, uses these tactics. It has enlisted 600 legislators to "oppose legislation relating to climate change that includes a net increase in government revenue."[191] The "pledge" that Americans for Prosperity promotes is considered an "antitax" pledge, although many of the proposals against which it is directed do not involve taxation. Later, we will see that specific proposals by some legislatures deal with policies such as the Regional Greenhouse Gas Initiative and other energy proposals devoid of taxation. Leaders of denial movements such as Americans for Prosperity tend to use disinformation such as "carbon tax" or phrases such as "cap and tax" to mislead followers.

Americans for Prosperity is funded by Koch Industries, the richest private company in the United States. Koch Industries is a major player in fossil fuel businesses, including oil refining, pipelines, and petrochemicals. As a fossil-fuel company, Koch Industries is interested in denial of climate change. Greenpeace identified the company as a "kingpin of climate science denial."[192] The Koch brothers, Charles and David, have also established foundations that contribute to many denial groups, including the Cato Institute, the Heritage Foundation, and Freedomworks. Freedomworks, formerly headed by former congressman Dick Armey, has organized many Tea Party events.

Tea Party activists and the "AstroTurf" movements such as Americans for Prosperity are linked. "Americans for Prosperity has worked closely with the Tea Party since the movement's inception."[193] In one survey, more than 70% of Tea Party adherents said there is no evidence of climate change.[194] These groups see their lifestyles threatened by regulation of energy to the detriment of personal choices in energy use. Radio and TV commentators such as Glenn Beck often stimulate them to attack climate science. For most members, the position of the groups on climate change is incidental to their position on other issues such as growth and government power.

While the denial movements have been operating for decades, starting with the "tobacco wars," their actions became more observable during 2011 and 2012. One effect of the denial movement is the influence it exerts on Congress. Often this is related to campaign contributions, as, for example, from Koch Industries to members of the House Energy and Commerce Committee, which has been pushing for limits on EPA regulation of greenhouse gases.[195] During debate on the Republican proposal to prevent the EPA from regulating GHG, Democratic Congressman Henry Waxman (previously chairman of the committee that supported cap-and-trade legislation in 2009) described Koch Industries' role: "The Koch brothers, I think, are unique, because they're not just interested in their financial well-being; they're interested in ideology. They are uniquely involved in the right wing of this country. They are financing the Tea Party movement and the Republican Party, and they're making the politics pay off for them both ideologically and economically."[196]

Americans for Prosperity became involved in the congressional debate on EPA regulations. It sent a memo to senators to solicit support for a proposal by Senate Minority Leader Mitch McConnell to nullify EPA greenhouse gas regulations.[197] If the congressional action succeeds in restricting EPA regulations, it will inhibit the only national climate policy currently in effect in the United States. Even without action in the Senate, the proposal has had a dampening effect on administration policy by making the EPA more cautious in implementing GHG emission regulations.

All denial groups rely on an inherent advantage of denial ideology: the tendency to disbelieve something that is uncomfortable or inconvenient to people's lifestyles. They exploit the feeling of discomfort with scientific findings that seem to contradict their values.[198] The scientific arguments for climate change can actually lead to strengthening the tendencies to believe in denial ideology among people who try to maintain their mind-set of denial, a prime example of the operation of mechanisms to reduce cognitive dissonance. Dissemination of climate science can backfire and cause people to become more tenacious deniers.[199]

As Upton Sinclair said, "It is difficult to get a man to understand something when his salary depends upon his not understanding it!" The denial movement uses cognitive dissonance between climate change facts and prosperity/energy values to convince people that it is not feasible to maintain their standard of living with climate policies that "threaten" this standard of living. The resolution of the dissonance is to deny the need for any policies by denying the science.

So what difference does it make that a small percentage of the population denies climate science? When this small percentage is highly committed to their views, it can have a major influence on the rest of society.[200] Anthony Leiserowitz confirms this interpretation. Although only about 10% of respondents in his surveys are "dismissive" of climate change, they can have a disproportionate influence on public policy. Even though denial ideology impels only a small percentage of people to engage in climate issues, they can "dominate much of the public square."[201] People who are motivated by denial ideology are strong enough in their beliefs to dismiss any evidence to the contrary of the ideology. Their strong beliefs propel them to make statements that influence others, such as the "doubtful" members of the public, distorting the message of climate science.

Denial movements often use the framework of "us versus them." In other words, ideology can be framed as an "in" group fighting "out" groups, conspiracies, or sometimes the whole world. Sometimes a movement may pose as an alternative to the social environment, providing opposing models for elites and myths of the surrounding society.[202] What, exactly, is the "them" that denial ideology opposes? Superficially, climate scientists or environmentalists can be seen as the "enemies," and one does encounter conspiracy theories about climate science in the ideology. More fundamentally, however, denial ideology sees the reality of climate change itself as the "thing" to be opposed. While many denial ideologues will admit that the climate is changing and may even argue forcefully that these changes are natural, they cannot bring themselves to face the facts about human-induced climate change. Climate change is telling us that increases in GHG emissions are profoundly altering our environment at a rapid pace that may become uncontrollable. This uncomfortable reality is the thing that denial ideologues oppose most vociferously. The scientists are merely the bearers of the bad messages and, like unfortunate message bearers of ancient Greece, may become the innocent victims of denial movements.

In conclusion, the denial movements embody the crux of issues involved in denial ideology. They develop the concepts and promulgate the ideas that form the core of the ideology. They use ideology to frame the debate on climate policies. Drawing on contrarian ideas about climate science, the movements purport to show that emission controls are not necessary and are, in fact, harmful to economic growth and job creation. They often succeed in convincing politicians and the public by raising doubt about climate science and calling for "balanced" presentation of positions. We will see in the next two chapters all of the spinoffs of the ideology that have influenced politics and public opinion.

Chapter 3.
Dynamics of Denial Ideology

Specific groups described in chapter 2 have unique themes in their ideologies, but there are more general themes that appear in denial ideology that transcend these groups. In this chapter we examine the underlying rationales for denial ideology, including the ethical arguments, growth, and capitalism.

Clichés such as "business as usual," "if it ain't broke, don't fix it," or "more of the same" illustrate the approach of denial ideology in response to climate change. Ironically, the phrase "business as usual" also has become a term of art for projecting scenarios of climate change. It implies that economic growth will continue on a path with steadily increasing GHG emissions. The implication is that if this growth extends very far into the future, consequences of climate change will worsen and truncate the very growth that is anticipated by denial ideologues.

Having denied climate science, ideologues look forward to continuous development of the world economy based on growth in fossil fuel consumption. Neither the prospect of resource depletion nor the consequences of global warming are factored into views of the future. Growth will gradually make things "better and better" along the same lines as the recent past. Denial ideologues tend to have a "ratchet" mentality when it comes to growth: at each stage, wealth and prosperity increase but never decrease. When consequences of climate change become evident, this view is likely to lead to cognitive dissonance, as the natural basis of prosperity comes under strain. Droughts and infrastructure failures (e.g., closing the Mississippi to barge traffic), such as those that occurred in the United States in 2012,[203] will set back economic growth and cause social strains.

Climate science is denigrated, for example, as "junk science" whenever it projects deleterious changes in the future.[204] Any hints of a possible change in direction other than the linear continuation of the present are dismissed. Cognitive dissonance does not permit admission of facts such as melting ice or sea level rise. When these phenomena occur, as they already have, the facts are rejected.

Ironically, the denial approach to change reverses the French aphorism "The more things change, the more they stay the same." With respect to climate change, the more things stay on the same track, the more they will change in the future. Continuous growth will lead to major unnatural changes that will severely impact societies.

In systems terms, the denial ideology definition of growth is likely to lead to overshoot and collapse. The current trajectory of economic growth (see below) will lead to depletion of resources, particularly energy, and climate problems will become more severe. While substitutes can be found for some resources, not all can be managed with technology. Technical solutions do not adequately address the overshoot and collapse issue, because there is no "technological substitute for soil and water."[205]

As economic and natural environments become less and less able to sustain growth, denial ideologues will become increasingly desperate and unable to maintain their leadership. The denial movements will eventually wither away as their leaders disappear from the media scene. Their influence will linger on, however, as the delays they induce in mitigation and adaptation exacerbate the inability of social and economic systems to cope with climate change.[206]

As climate change effects become more widespread and harder to avoid, denial movements may become more radical in fighting the facts. Denial movements may try to "hold the line" and keep growth on a path of continuity. Nature will not stand still for them, however, and the reactions of denial advocates may become more and more fearful as climate change consequences become more severe. For some in the denial movement, one reaction is to heap up denials with a series of canards about climate change.[207] These include such familiar themes as "the world is cooling, not warming," "climate science is highly uncertain," and "carbon dioxide does not cause warming." In this vein, denial ideology plays on the fears of the future implicit in scenarios projected by climate science.

The Cornwall Alliance unwittingly reveals its motives for climate denial: the fear that people will be "haunted" by concerns about global warming means that the denial message will be rejected.[208] The Cornwall Alliance uses one of the major tactics of denial movements: suppression of fear through denial of the facts. This is a classic example of cognitive dissonance at work. While we may prefer to deny climate change, we will not be able to avoid its consequences. Eventually nature wins.

One way of looking at the interaction of ideology and social change is to analyze the different effects of cognitive dissonance in reaction to climate change. Most of the leaders and many members of denial movements will attempt to maintain their denial beliefs in reaction to climate change, denying the reality of events to the point where their world views become quite brittle. They may reach a breaking point when their ideology is completely discredited and the movement loses credibility. A particularly dynamic change of social movements is the possibility of members moving from one type to another, and even whole groups shifting course. Thus denial movements may lose members or reorient their rhetoric as the effects of climate change become more obvious. We would expect that the social dynamics observed by Festinger et al.[209] would also hold true for denial movements. As they noted, leaders in movements with ideologies that contradict reality will try to maintain their beliefs despite disproof, but members may leave the movement, leaving only a hard core of true believers.

Ethical Dimensions of Denial Ideology

Denial movements view unfettered economic growth as an ethical imperative. This view supports the judgment that governments should not constrain the use of fossil fuels, which are needed to promote growth. Lomborg expresses this judgment in his call for eradication of poverty and disease through economic growth, an ethical judgment based on his view that poverty and disease are more immediate and significant threats.[210] Such a view is typical of denial ideologues who pose a false dichotomy between resolving poverty and climate change. It is false on two counts: solutions to the two problems are complementary, not contradictory; and ignoring climate change will make poverty worse in the long run. This false dichotomy is also embraced by the Cornwall Alliance, which says, "We believe mandatory reductions in carbon dioxide and other greenhouse gas emissions, achievable mainly by greatly reduced use of fossil fuels, will greatly increase the price of energy and harm economies." Its denial argument is then extended to claim that climate policies will harm the poor more than others.[211]

In this point of view, any reduction in fossil fuel use for energy is immoral because it means that societies will change for the worse. The statement assumes that there are no substitutes for fossil fuels, and that economies cannot grow without their use. This is a rather narrow view of the future. Where do these ethical views originate?

It can be said that such judgments are ethical principles applied to events and reality. The origin of these ethical principles can be science, religion, or beliefs derived from science and religion. When these beliefs are expressed as ideologies, they often take the form of prescriptive rules. For example, religions might propose that God's will determines the fate of the earth and that man cannot thwart this will: "The earth will end only when God declares it's time to be over. Man will not destroy this earth" (Rep. John Shimkus, R-IL).[212] Sen. James Inhofe (R-OK) has a similar view: "My point is, God's still up there. The arrogance of people to think that we human beings would be able to change what he is doing in the climate is to me outrageous."[213]

Many fundamentalists tend to argue that only God will determine the future. A Kentucky state senator, Stan Lee, said, "The climate's always going to change. We're not in control of this world…There is one who is in control, but it ain't any of us. And to think that we can change what he created, I think, is shortsighted and foolish."[214] Such views originate in the Noah flood story in the Bible, when God promised Noah not to flood the earth again. They seem to reflect a fundamentalist belief that God would not let humans endanger the earth, but God may not be so tolerant of human foibles.

Other members of Congress express similar sentiments. Rep. Todd Rokita (R-IN) has said, "I think it's arrogant that we think as people that we can somehow change the climate of the whole earth when science is telling us that there's a cycle to all this. And that cycle was occurring before the Industrial Revolution and I suspect will occur way into the future."[215] This more secular view of climate change removes causation from human agency. It reflects the fundamentalist view that humans are somehow separate from nature.

Ideology generally has a set of fixed premises and conclusions derived from those premises. If ideologies are derived from nonempirical beliefs such as religion, they can be inherently unstable, since the beliefs may lead to assumptions about the physical world that are not supported by events. An example is the concept of "God's intelligent design of ecosystems" that are sustainable on their own because they are "resilient, self-regulating, and self-correcting."[216] This viewpoint tends to regard natural processes as separate from human activities, and therefore not subject to anthropogenic influences such as greenhouse gas emissions. If physical events or trends undermine the "biblical world view of godly dominion over earth,"[217] the contradiction raises questions about the underlying religious beliefs. In other words, deriving an ideology from religious beliefs and applying judgments to the empirical world involves both the risk of disproof of the ideology and abandonment of the underlying religious beliefs. This makes the ideology inherently unstable and subject to disavowal by disillusioned adherents.

The Cornwall Alliance takes this a step further by blaming environmentalists for a world view that does not subordinate nature to man and God. It advocates a "biblical world view of godly dominion over the earth."[218] Perhaps because environmentalists are concerned about how humans affect nature, they are not "biblical" enough in their world views. While asserting that a "biblical world view" enables "humanity and the natural world [to] thrive together," this view clearly puts God and humanity above nature.[219] Such a view would make denial more plausible; after all, any consequences of climate change could be interpreted as God's will rather than man's behavior. No change in human activities would be necessary.

The Cornwall Alliance folds in climate change with evolution as a package of science education that ignores "intelligent design," the new buzzwords for creationism.[220] Since intelligent design teaches that "man is not an accident of nature," but a purposely designed intelligent being, it also teaches that global warming is not possible since man and nature are not accidents. The Cornwall Alliance also argues that the increases in carbon dioxide are minuscule, "increasing carbon dioxide from 27 to 54 thousandths of 1% (270 to 540 parts per million)." Presumably, this means that CO2 concentrations will have no effect on climate, and efforts to refute denialism are *argumentum ad baculum*, which means argument by force or coercion. In other words, climate science is viewed as tyrannical because it seems to mandate social changes deemed undesirable by denial ideologues.

In contrast to these ideological views, science uses a different approach. Michael Mann, author of the "hockey stick" (see chapter 1), describes the ethical issues involved in climate science as "the legacy that we want to leave our children and grandchildren." He notes that "the fossil fuels that we're burning, the emissions resulting from our behavior today, are influencing the climate for decades and even centuries into the future."[221] Many scientists have an ethical view of how to approach the fate of the earth. While scientific findings do not expressly promote ethical judgments, the view that fossil fuel emissions will destroy the biosphere can be derived from climate science.[222] Scientists do not inherently reject the proposition that poverty and disease are priority issues, and they also do not assert that climate is a higher or lower priority. An ethical case can be made for making climate issues equally high priorities if the consequences of climate change, e.g., drought and floods, are so severe as to wipe out all of the benefits of sustainable development.[223] Analysis of climate change as an influence on social change puts into perspective the moral dimension of emissions control. Many of the historic sources of emissions are in rich countries, while many of the vulnerable people are in developing countries. "The world's poor people are disproportionately vulnerable to loss of livelihood and assets, dislocation, hunger, and famine in the face of climate variability and change."[224]

Millennium Development Goals (MDG) are closely related to climate change; they include food security, clean water, and eradication of poverty and disease, all of which are threatened by climate change. All UN members subscribe to the MDG, but their realization is undermined by current patterns of economic growth associated with increased rates of greenhouse gas emissions growth. This conundrum has been the ethical basis for the principle of common but differentiated responsibility for emissions reductions. The Kyoto Protocol embodied this principle by distinguishing between "Annex I" parties (the United States, Japan, Australia, New Zealand, Western Europe, Eastern Europe, and the former Soviet Republics) and "non-Annex I" (developing) parties. Annex I parties committed to an average of 5% emissions reductions from 1990 to 2012. Nearly all of the Annex I countries except the United States ratified the Kyoto Protocol; the United States objected on the basis that non-Annex I countries such as China, India, and Brazil do not have quotas and have faster emissions growth than Annex I countries. This issue remains a major sticking point in negotiations under the UN Framework Convention on Climate Change. Ethics tends to clash with economics in these negotiations, but the two are not necessarily diametric opposites.

Many observers have noted that addressing poverty, disease, and climate change can be done with complementary policies that mitigate all three.[225] United Nations Environment Program (UNEP) Executive Director Achim Steiner has made the connection:

> The green economy—as documented and illustrated in the
> [UNEP] report—offers a focused and pragmatic assessment

of how countries, communities, and corporations have begun to make a transition toward a more sustainable pattern of consumption and production...Development cannot come at the expense of the very life support systems on land, in the oceans, or in the atmosphere that sustain our economies and, thus, the lives of each and every one of us.[226]

If other priorities are elevated above climate mitigation and adaptation, policies to address climate change may be delayed or watered down. This reinforces the approach taken by the denial movement when it is unable to refute findings of climate science. By invoking ethical concerns with jobs, poverty, disease, and other more immediate problems, the movement plays upon the anxieties of the public as a justification to delay or deny the need for energy policies.

Some denial ideologues seek to blame climate scientists for promoting poverty and other "sins" of climate science. "There is no convincing evidence that anyone has ever been killed by manmade global warming. But we have daily evidence that poverty kills."[227] It is disputable that "there is no convincing evidence that anyone has ever been killed by man-made global warming," when analysts estimate that 300,000 people die each year from the effects of global warming.[228] To call the threat "theoretical" when there is already evidence of droughts and floods that have killed people is also tendentious and ethically questionable. Whether denial is motivated by ethical or crass concerns, the effect is the same. Delay in addressing climate change will exacerbate the very problems that denial advocates claim to address through growth.

Gardiner offers a different view of ethical behavior: "Not only is it the case that we can pass the buck onto the poor, the future, and nature, but we face strong temptations to do so. This makes us ethically vulnerable. One way in which we may succumb is to refuse to acknowledge that there is problem at all."[229] In other words, denial is a response to challenges to our morality, involving a corruption of ethics through "temptations to pass the buck." While we may believe that we are behaving ethically by delaying low-carbon energy policies in order to solve other problems first, the opposite is true. The delay of climate policies may result in problems that overwhelm all of the other efforts to resolve poverty, disease, and inequality.

Issues of morality spotlight the deep divide between denial and climate science. While climate scientists grapple with the problems of the real world, denial ideologues construct a fantasy world in which humans have dominion over the earth. Scientists try to determine the resource limits to growth, while ideologues believe that there are no limits to what humans can do. The crux of the problem is the issue of growth.

Growth

Growth is a major issue in climate change denial ideology. Growth brings out social and environmental issues that affect the ideologies of social movements. It is fraught with risks. If you support growth policies, as nearly every government must, you risk the consequences for the environment, as China's experience demonstrates. If you oppose growth, you will be shunned by the electorate and most economists. Even if you qualify support by calling for "sustainable" growth, you open a can of worms because of fundamental disagreements about the definition of *sustainable*.

Whenever growth is uneven, as it usually is, there are issues of wealth distribution. Whenever growth impacts the environment, it raises issues of viability. In regard to climate change, growth raises the issue of energy use and its impact on global warming. Sometimes the issues are stated as "progrowth" or "antigrowth," but this vastly oversimplifies the ideological issues.

It is glib to say that growth can continue on track by switching away from fossil fuels, when problems of scale and reliability plague alternative energy technologies. It is a little more realistic to say that growth can be channeled into sustainable paths, but there is always the problem of living standards. Not only are Europe, the United States,

Japan, etc., at high levels of consumption, but also many emerging economies are trying to catch up. If growth is to continue, this issue must be addressed.

North America is particularly reliant on fossil fuels to energize growth. It would not be an exaggeration to say that US prosperity relies largely on fossil fuel use. "For a country that has traditionally used its cheap supply of energy to substitute for more expensive labor and capital costs to compete internationally, this linkage is particularly strong, as witnessed by the nation's high GHG emissions per capita."[230]

One reason that denial ideology has found fertile soil in the United States is this close interrelationship. Without the "cheap" energy from fossil fuels, costs per unit of production would be much higher, and growth rates would be much lower. Energy is cheap only because it is priced well below true costs; in other words, the costs of energy are "externalized" to the environment. This economic fact leads to the issues of growth versus environment that denial ideologues exploit.

Denial movements tend to view growth as an unblemished good. Unfettered growth is the core of denial myths and beliefs; growth is built into the rationale of current economic and social systems. On the other hand, growth does have consequences beyond changes in income or resource use. Most of these consequences stem from the physical limits of economic systems that, when exceeded, result in "overshoot and collapse."[231] *Overshoot* is a term used by systems analysts to indicate that economic growth has its limits, a subject of intense debate. Many critics have pointed out that the emphasis on limits overstates the issue of growth versus environment. Changes since *Limits to Growth* was first published in the 1970s have called into question the application of the concept to contemporary society. Increases in supplies of energy, such as shale gas, and oil, have removed some of the limits. Nevertheless, the concept of overshoot still applies to climate change: "The Global Footprint Network has estimated that because of population growth, humans globally consume 50% more resources each year than can be sustained by natural systems. This means we are eating into the natural capital that makes the planet habitable. Climate change is just one measure of this 'overshoot.' "[232]

The direction of growth, its effects with respect to use of resources and sustainability, is the major environmental issue raised by this school of thinking. Principal among the uses of resources is the dependence of growth on fossil fuels. With climate change, this growth will have serious problems of overshoot in the 21st century. Energy use as a resource must in any case decline from present levels. "The oil companies, private and state owned, have current reserves on the books equivalent to 2,795 gigatons—five times more than we can ever safely burn. It has to stay in the ground."[233] Climate change is likely to accelerate at a rate that will overwhelm any transition due to oil depletion. The more basic issue is the rate and nature of economic growth.

One of the main issues about growth in the context of climate change is what kind of growth is measured. Gross domestic production (GDP) measures all increases in spending, including activities responding to environmental disasters and causing damage to ecosystems, even though those are not net increases in welfare. Some economists, such as Herman Daly, have termed these measurements "uneconomic growth." "I contend that we have reached the economic limit to growth but we don't know it, and desperately hide the fact by faulty national accounting because growth is our idol and to stop worshiping it is anathema."[234]

Current paradigms of growth continue to rely in assumptions of continuous increases in wealth, and it is difficult to change that trajectory. Speaking of growth in the Southwest United States, deBuys makes a crucial point: "Growth must be limited; the train must be stopped. But who is willing to stand on the tracks and flag it down? The economy of the region is predicated on continuous growth."[235] Climate scientists and environmentalists hesitate to stand on the tracks to flag down the train. Too many of them have been run over.[236]

One of the problems of growth is the way it is measured. Gross domestic product, or GDP, measures growth only in terms of the additions of products and services to national wealth. In a way, climate can be viewed as one of the resources not reflected in GDP measurement. The stability of the world's climate is one of those "natural capital stocks" that is overlooked in growth measurements. Some authors have argued that the atmosphere is a "scarce" resource, one that should be treated the same in economic models as any other scarce resource such as energy or metal ores.[237]

A more serious consideration of growth for the analysis of climate change is the comparison of the costs of growth with or without emissions reductions. Emissions costs will reduce the benefits of growth proportionally. An analysis that uses a comparison of costs of "damages," or consequences of climate change, shows the costs of damages by 2100 are approximately $10 trillion with climate policies that cost about $2 trillion. Without these policies, the costs will double by 2100 and nearly triple by 2200.[238] In other words, for an investment of $2 trillion, the return is five times as much environmental improvement.

There are other estimates of costs, and they vary according to the definitions and assumptions used. Stern has calculated "a figure of around $85 billion per annum by 2015 as representing the extra costs arising from a more hostile climate." He uses a variety of calculations and factors, including droughts, floods, and other impacts on agriculture and infrastructure. He goes on to say, "But what is very clear is that these costs are on the order of scores of billions of dollars per annum in the next decade or two. They would rise very rapidly into the many trillions if climate change is not managed sensibly."[239]

Ultimately, economists' treatment of growth becomes an issue of decision making based on public opinion. When posed in this fashion, the issue puts climate policies at a disadvantage. According to Roger Pielke, "When policies on emissions reductions collide with policies focused on economic growth, economic growth will win out every time."[240] Perhaps it would be more accurate to say that economic growth will win out in the near term but lose in the long term.

Pielke's point is well taken, but the crucial issue is *how* climate policies flow with the current of public opinion. That is difficult to manage, as public opinion varies considerably with rates of growth (or shrinkage, as has been the case in recent years) and priorities shift. Where growth occurs, that is, which sectors grow more or less, is also a crucial issue: renewable energy can add as much to growth as other forms of energy.

Unbridled growth is likely to lead to collapse. "Collapse" is a term used by Jared Diamond to describe environmental disasters that have befallen a number of societies in the past.[241] His analysis of Easter Island, Norse Greenland, and Mayan civilization, among others, illustrates the interrelationship of unfettered growth in the use of resources, overshoot, and collapse. He also shows, in the case of Tokugawa, Japan, how growth can be controlled and some of the worst consequences reversed. While Diamond does not apply his analysis directly to growth in the use of fossil fuels and its consequences for climate change, he provides a framework for analysis of these issues.

The concept of limits to growth has spurred further analysis of the consequences of unfettered economic growth. Martenson summarizes the arguments involving growth and energy as "physical limits" that are not acknowledged by the economy, which requires growth to sustain jobs and service debts.[242] Modern technology and a high standard of living are "fueled" by fossil fuels, which have enabled modern society to attain a high level of growth during the past two centuries. This growth is the basis of a high standard of living in the United States and enables a car culture and suburban sprawl to define American society. Our use of fossil fuel supports this standard of living, although cutting energy use would not necessarily lower it: "An average American emits twice the CO_2 as the average European or Japanese. Cutting US emissions by half without sacrificing standard of living is demonstrably doable."[243]

The denial movement needs to reject the environmental implications of growth in order to maintain a belief in its unlimited benefits for human welfare. Adherents assert that growth will alleviate poverty and enhance social mobility. Because growth, particularly economic growth, is seen as the palliative to social and economic problems, as well as a key to personal wealth, many find questioning the premises of growth troubling enough to reject any alternative world view.

Since high living standards, convenient transportation and economic growth may depend on increasing supplies of fossil fuels, modern society is highly vulnerable to economic and environmental problems of energy. Modern society depends on petroleum because of its use in transportation and chemical products. Without enough oil for cars, trucks, and aircraft, and coal for generation of electricity, the world will shrink to more local levels, and growth will change direction when environmental limits are reached.[244]

The idea that reduction of energy use will mean a "smaller world" is a key issue in denial ideology. If fossil fuels become increasingly expensive, society will have to adapt by reducing the scope of travel and consumption. Reliance on local food and entertainment will be necessary; leisure travel will be restricted to nearby places; and commuting will change from single-occupancy vehicles to mass transit. All of these possibilities create major concerns for denial movements.

The current paradigm of economic growth, which depends on cheap energy, is likely to have problems when energy becomes more costly. Most societies are fueled by a combination of energy sources, including the oil and gas needed for agricultural production, transportation, and heating; and gas, nuclear energy, and coal for electricity production. When these sources become more expensive, the societies will experience economic change that can lead to social unrest.[245] Recent examples are the Middle East uprisings ignited by high food prices and unemployment.

When energy is priced higher, social and economic change will be inevitable. Living standards and freedom of movement may be limited, particularly for those dependent on fossil-fueled growth in housing, business, and transportation. Denial movements seek to deal with the cognitive dissonance of growth versus physical limits by denying the reality of the limits. The rationale for continuing expansion of energy demand is often built into the infrastructure and governance of the economy. Energy efficiency is one of the most effective ways to reduce energy demand without reducing living standards. If this is so obvious, why haven't more businesses and homeowners adopted energy efficiency? It is often that regulators and government rules favor high energy production with little or no incentives for efficiency.[246]

Continuing growth without changing energy policy will lead to climate problems. Leading economists have analyzed the possibilities of continuing growth on the current path or moving to a low-carbon economy. Nobel Laureate Joseph Stiglitz and Sir Nicholas Stern advised President Obama: "The investments necessary to convert our society to a low-carbon economy—investments that can change the way we live and work—would drive growth over the next two or three decades. They would ensure that growth, with accompanying improvements in standards of living, was sustainable. The path that we have been on now is not."[247]

Given that current trends are unsustainable, it is necessary to examine how society will respond to change. How movements will react to social changes resulting from climate change is problematic. History has examples of reactionary movements that become violent in defense of traditional values, e.g., the Spanish Inquisition, the Ku Klux Klan. While modern movements usually have more sophisticated responses, they may not be able to avoid violence as an "end game" in the progression of social change.

There is a tendency of denial movements to reject any suggestions that growth has limits and to cast aspersion on those who dare to suggest that problems result from current economic trends. "Those who suggest we may want to consider other slow-growth paths are shouted down as Luddites or environmental extremists or are dismissed as being ignorant of basic economics…or even as being 'anti-growth,' as if what we need is more growth."[248]

Growth of energy supplies is a major problem for the world, according to the International Energy Agency. Executive Director of the International Energy Agency Nobuo Tanaka noted: "The age of cheap energy is over. The only question now is, will the extra rent from dearer energy go to an ever smaller circle of producers, or will it be directed back into the domestic economies of the consumers, with the added benefits of increased environmental sustainability?"[249]

This raises two issues: how fossil fuels will be priced and distributed, and whether renewable energy and efficiency will come online soon enough to replace fossil fuels in part or whole. Who will pay for the growth in energy? The questions of fairness and sustainability are closely intertwined with energy prices and technologies. These issues drive the ideologies of social movements.

Based on assumptions that energy growth is limitless, conventional economics has developed concepts that rely on constant expansion of economies. When these concepts are challenged by finite physical limits, economic theory becomes a different approach. According to this view, growth is subject to four principles:

- Limits: "Growth in population and consumption rates cannot be sustained."
- Consumption: "Renewable resources must be consumed at rates below those of natural replenishment."
- Recycling: "Nonrenewable resources must be consumed at declining rates (with rates of decline at least equaling rates of depletion), and recycled wherever possible."
- Waste: "Wastes must be minimized, rendered nontoxic to humans and the environment, and made into 'food' for natural systems or human production processes."[250]

These four principles have major implications for economic models of growth. If implemented, they would require a major change in the assumptions about markets and societies.

One major problem is the existing paradigm of growth, based on constant expansion of resource use and development with little regard for energy efficiency. While some technological advances have reduced energy use per unit of production, these efficiencies have been overtaken by the rapid growth of consumption. Even if autos have higher mileage, for example, the growth in numbers (e.g., China) and mileage driven overtakes the savings in fuel. This is known as the Jevons paradox, after a 19th-century English economist who first developed it.

The use of wind power, the reduction of energy costs per unit of production, and other "sets of equation" will be principal issues of future energy use. Measurement of efficiencies and sustainability of resources will be the driving factors, not growth per se. Some authors have proposed specific, practical measures of efficiencies, including "grading" buildings and appliances and projecting total energy costs for major purchases, such as autos, appliances, and homes.[251]

One of the major issues for environmental policy is population growth. Its effects on climate change and biodiversity were addressed by the Center for Biological Diversity, which promoted a program of population control to preserve biodiversity. This led to a number of political and public opinion problems because of the sensitivity of population issues. Growth in population not only damages habitats that can provide ecological services, but it affects climate change. A study by the National Academy of Sciences "showed how slowing the country's population growth rate to 1.5 births per woman from 2.0 could result in a 10% drop in greenhouse gas emissions by midcentury and a 33% drop by the end of the century."[252] That would seem to be straight mathematical projection of current trends, but it aroused the ire of denial ideologues. When Oregon State University released a study in 2009 calculating the extra carbon dioxide emissions a person helps generate by choosing to have children, the researchers received hate mail labeling them "eugenicists" and "Nazis."[253]

Once again, we see that any discussion of growth triggers strong emotions and crowds out rational decision making. Addressing population growth along with economic growth doubles the risk of attacks from denial ideologues. More likely than any specific policies are economic and political changes, where social movements seek to deal with environmental constraints through collective action. In the short term, denial movements will seek to adapt to escalating resource costs with escalating claims to resources. Inflation is a likely concomitant to resource depletion, and denial movements tend to blame inflation on government policies rather than market forces.

Social movements develop ideologies when beliefs about reality are dissonant with the reality of change, and the movements address this dissonance by trying to change reality. Growth is one of the methods that movements attempt to use, for example, to improve members' lives or to overcome social problems related to resource scarcity. Growth itself implies movement, including social mobility, but the direction of growth and how it is managed are critical factors in its success. Growth based on unsustainable use of resources in the short term may make it difficult to sustain favorable change in the long term. Conservation of resources implies a different type of growth, a paradigm shift toward a different lifestyle and economic system. This shift will be resisted by those who want to maintain their prerogatives.[254]

Analysis of growth is further complicated by its tendency to polarize opinions and put ideological blinders on analysts. Stern indicates that leftist ideologues put a high priority on poverty and overlook the need for low-carbon growth that will support sustainable development. Rightist ideologues are more concerned about avoiding regulation and fail to see the market failures of "free" capitalism. Growth must be analyzed independent of leftist or rightist ideology, or its implications for the future will be misunderstood.[255]

Ideological conflict over growth occurs within the profession of economics between neoliberals who rely on the market and Keynesians who call for government action. But both of these schools of thought may be missing some essential points. Growth is limited, whatever the philosophical basis of economics that posits unlimited growth. It is egregious to analyze growth without taking into account the natural basis of economies.[256] Even if the arguments of peak oil are dismissed, growth will still encounter other limits, including mineral resources, land use (including depletion of nutrients), and population problems.

Growth and Capitalism

Questions about the issue of growth in relation to climate change inevitably lead to questions about capitalism. As the dominant economic model of the 21st century, capitalism will have a major role to play in the future of Earth's climate. Some observers think that the ethical conundrum of growth versus environment can be overcome through education and changes in the capitalist system,[257] but others think that capitalism will lead to environmental catastrophe unless priorities are reversed.[258] The ethical issue of growth involves a particular ideology of capitalism, sometimes expressed as a purist view of the market system. "Pure" capitalist ideology often promotes "free" market mechanisms, which are threatened by "environmentalism."[259] Some commentators go even further and accuse climate science of destroying industrial society.[260]

Of course, these critiques target environmentalists and "ecozealots" using stereotypes of activists who try to address broad issues of climate change and society. There are more specific issues about the role of capitalism in climate change that come to the fore when regulation of greenhouse gases is proposed. Such views are often invoked by opponents of EPA regulation of greenhouse gases, such as Rep. Fred Upton (R-MI) and Sen. James Inhofe (R-OK). They tend to argue that any regulation of greenhouse gases (GHG) will destroy the economy. Of course, they have other motives as well, stemming from their views that climate change is not "necessarily" due to anthropogenic GHG (Upton) or that climate change is "the greatest hoax ever perpetrated on the American people" (Inhofe). In this respect members of Congress express the views of the denial movement, especially the Tea Party, on whom they depend for support. More analysis of these trends can be found in chapter 4.

Among denial ideologues, capitalism and growth are cornerstones of their rejection of climate science and environmental activism. Two leading ideologues, James Delingpole of Britain and Joseph Bast of the Heartland Institute, have used anticapitalism as a basis of their critiques: "Climate change is the perfect thing…It's the reason why we should do everything [the left] wanted to do anyway."[261]

Issues of taxes, regulation, redistribution of wealth, and government intervention are potent themes for many denial advocates. While scientists, diplomats, and business leaders try to grapple with the pragmatic problems of energy use, ideologues flail out with accusations that go way beyond the immediate questions of emissions and economic growth. In this manner, they attempt to capture the attention of people who may not be threatened by the science or even some of the proposed solutions, but who can be manipulated by emotional arguments.

An argument about jobs reverberates throughout the denial literature. It is usually only an assertion about the loss of "millions of jobs"; seldom are the jobs specifically identified by industry. In fact, there is much more substance to counterarguments about job creation; these arguments often identify specific jobs and sectors that will increase with scaling up alternative energy.[262]

Another issue is whether climate policies will cost more than "business as usual" because they might require enormous investments in efficiency and renewable energy. Some denial advocates assert that these costs would lower average incomes of Americans, but the data indicate otherwise.[263] Benefits from reducing emissions of greenhouse gases will exceed costs by a wide margin.

Measuring costs and benefits is a complicated issue. Many of the immediate costs are measured in terms of investments needed to build an economy based on alternative energies, while the benefits are measured in terms of long-term savings (economic and environmental) from reduced fossil fuel energy use. The "capitalist" view of climate change sometimes takes the form of arguing that even if climate science is accurate, the short-term costs of controlling emissions far outweigh the long-term benefits. The *Wall Street Journal* editorialized: "What we don't know is exactly how sensitive the climate is to increases in these gases versus other possible factors—solar variability, oceanic currents, Pacific heating and cooling cycles, planets' gravitational and magnetic oscillations, and so on." Note that the editorial couples uncertainty about greenhouse gas emissions with uncertainty about other climate influences, a dubious association at best. The editorial then goes on to conclude, "Given the unknowns, it's possible that even if we spend trillions of dollars, and forgo trillions more in future economic growth, to cut carbon emissions to preindustrial levels, the climate will continue to change—as it always has."[264] It is a specious argument to link two different types of "unknowns" and conclude that both have the same effect.

The *Wall Street Journal* repeats a number of denial canards. Asserting that "we don't know exactly how sensitive the climate is to increases" in greenhouse gases, the statement ignores a whole series of studies that document climate sensitivity to greenhouse gases.[265] By downgrading the certainty of climate science, this argument assumes that economic growth should continue unhindered because there are "unknown" consequences of climate change, when we know with a great deal of certainty that there are serious consequences already under way. Perhaps the most egregious is that it is better to maintain "known" (i.e., predicted) economic growth than worry about "unknown" (i.e., projected) costs of climate change. Defending capitalism by repeating these canards about growth does not serve capitalism well.

The *Wall Street Journal* is sometimes viewed as a prime voice for capitalism. As such, it has a tendency to print denial statements and ignore climate science.[266] On one occasion, the *Wall Street Journal* found 16 "so-called experts" to sign its op-ed piece and attacked the scientists who disagreed with the sixteen, accusing them of "alarmism" and greed.[267] The 16 "experts" included some of the denial ideologues described in chapter 1. The National Academy of Sciences sent a letter that read, in part: "WE ARE DEEPLY DISTURBED BY THE RECENT ESCALATION OF POLITICAL ASSAULTS ON SCIENTISTS in general and on climate scientists in particular…For a problem as potentially catastrophic as climate change, taking no action poses a dangerous risk for our planet."[268] (Emphasis in original.)

Scientists who signed the letter were all members of the National Academy of Sciences and included Nobel Prize winners such as Paul Crutzen.

Instead of the letter from the NAS the *Wall Street Journal* printed an op-ed article, which reads in part: "The lack of warming for more than a decade—indeed, the smaller-than-predicted warming over the 22 years since the U.N.'s Intergovernmental Panel on Climate Change

(IPCC) began issuing projections—suggests that computer models have greatly exaggerated how much warming additional CO2 can cause… The fact is that CO2 is not a pollutant. CO2 is a colorless and odorless gas, exhaled at high concentrations by each of us, and a key component of the biosphere's life cycle."[269]

Two canards are included in this statement: "lack of warming for more than a decade," and "CO2 is not a pollutant." As we have seen earlier, the decade 2000–2010 was the warmest on record, and the Clean Air Act defines CO2 as a pollutant, a definition confirmed by a 2007 Supreme Court ruling. The *Wall Street Journal* chooses to use these canards, perhaps to simplify its arguments and appeal to readers who want to believe that unhindered economic growth will have no effect on climate.

Attacks on scientists who raise questions about current models of growth continue. A Massachusetts Institute of Technology scientist, Kerry Emanuel, was attacked when he made a presentation on climate science to the New Hampshire Republican "Climate Hawks." He described the aftermath as follows:

> I think most of my colleagues and I have received a fair bit of e-mail here and there that you might classify as 'hate mail,' but nothing like what I've got in the last few days. What was a little bit new about it was dragging family members into it and feeling that my family might be under threat, so naturally I didn't feel very good about that at all. I thought it was low to drag somebody's spouse into arguments like this.[270]

Polarization of opinions about climate change has reached the point where climate scientists are receiving hate mail and denial ideologues are making threats against family members as well as the climate scientists themselves. Perhaps the fear of threats to economic growth and living standards has reached the level of extremism. The most egregious example of this fear is a book titled *Agenda 21*.[271] The author imagines that any of the policies proposed to control climate change will involve dispossession from the United Nations. He fantasizes a number of other deleterious threats from international actions on climate change. Inhofe uses similar appeals to fear.[272] One reason denial ideologues use fear as a tactic is to close off understanding of climate science and lead people to shut their minds to the consequences of climate change.

Polarization is paradoxical: it can be bolstered by both information and misinformation. Those who are more informed about an issue would tend to take one side, i.e., the assertion that climate change is anthropogenic and dangerous. By the same token, those who are more misinformed about the issue consider themselves equally qualified to assert that climate change is solely natural and not dangerous. This bifurcation of opinions tends to drive positions on the issue further apart.[273]

Science literacy, as mentioned in the preface, is no guarantee of accurate knowledge about climate change. It is, however, a means of arguing about the issue based on either correct information or misinformation; the choice is based on "cultural polarization." This form of polarization is driven by group affiliation, or "beliefs in line with those held by others with whom they share close ties." Group affiliation, in turn, is often driven by economic interests and ideas about economic growth.

The assumption of unhindered economic growth is a dangerous assumption, given the projected costs of effects of climate change—for example, up to 20% of world GDP.[274] The costs of reducing emissions will also increase as societies delay implementing climate policies: "[James] Hansen said that if we wait 10 years to begin reducing greenhouse gas emissions, we will need to reduce them at a rate of 15% per year to stabilize the climate. This, he said, would be 'difficult and expensive—perhaps impossible.'"[275]

The certainty of economic growth is considerably lower than the certainty of climate change costs. There is already evidence of economic consequences of climate change,[276] while projections of long-term economic growth are tendentious at best. William Nordhaus, whose work has sometimes been cited by denial ideologues to "prove" that climate policies can wait, makes the opposite point. His research shows that efficiency and other measures to reduce CO_2 emissions should be undertaken now and that waiting "is not only economically costly, but will also make the transition much more costly when it eventually takes place."[277] Nordhaus reinforces a major point about the economics of climate change: waiting to implement climate policies will increase costs significantly. This point is often lost in discussions by denial ideologues who cite Nordhaus for their arguments on cost.

Notwithstanding his clear statement in favor of strong action now, Nordhaus's work has sometimes been misused but other economists have argued that strong action can be delayed. This has fed into denial ideology.[278] Nicholas Stern calls for a broader perspective than the usual "utility function" of economic models in the analysis of climate change. He notes the need for ethical judgments on the value of different policies and outcomes used in the models and cautions against some of the common "discount" concepts used for projections.

Denial ideologues attack climate science for its uncertainties, but the certainty of the kind of economic growth they promote, based on "free" markets, is much lower. A different view of market economics is offered by Joseph Stiglitz, a Nobel Prize economist.[279] Stiglitz's point about market signals is a crucial one for the sound long-term operation of capitalist markets. If the markets fail to price in the long-term costs of climate change and resource depletion, they will drive capitalism into a disastrous dead end.

Market signals are price signals, and the current pricing system tends to send the wrong messages. They tend to ignore the enormous value of ecosystem services and "natural capital." "Natural capital" is ecosystem services provided by nature—including things like water purification in forests and wetlands, soil regeneration by microbes and legumes, and moderate rainfall. With regard to climate, these services include the sequestration of carbon by plants and absorption of carbon by oceans. When we overlook these natural processes in our calculations, we are risking "irrevocable damage to $33 trillion worth of natural capital."[280] Where did this number come from? Economist Robert Costanza and associates calculated this number using a broad definition of natural resources. It is a number that is very difficult to estimate using traditional economic analysis, but we ignore it at our peril.

It is sometimes necessary to go beyond economics to calculate costs of climate change. Because of doctrines of "other things being equal" (*ceteris paribus*) or the disregard of "externalities," conventional economics cannot measure true costs. Ultimately, climate change is a "crisis of capitalism" because it affects "business as usual" growth so adversely.[281] Economic crises such as the 2008 recession are signals of the problems of capitalism. At a more fundamental level, there are issues of wealth. Martenson analyzes wealth as primary (natural resources), secondary (goods and services produced from natural resources), and tertiary (stocks, bonds, money, and other claims on primary and secondary wealth). He notes that tertiary wealth depends heavily on growth, which is limited by natural resources.[282] Whether capitalism is viewed as a cause of climate problems or not, it is a prevalent economic system in the world. Even China, nominally communist, is behaving as a capitalist society. The question is, how will capitalism confront climate problems?

The most radical critique of capitalism contends that it cannot, by its very nature, sustain society in the face of climate change. Capitalism, according to this view, depends on continuous growth and exploitation of natural resources at an ever-expanding scale until it leads to collapse. "The economic development of capitalism has always carried with it social and ecological degradation—an ecological curse."[283] In the end, this may be the only critique left standing, but it tends to feed the denial ideology by playing on fears of Marxism or communism.

If we rely on ideology for our narrative of growth, whether capitalism, communism, or climate denial, we are going to run into the limitations of nature. Growth must be ideologically neutral and built upon the recognition of the natural processes that sustain our lives and our civilization.

As this analysis and review of literature has indicated, capitalism has numerous implications for climate change. There is no one clear model of growth that can be purely tied to either promoting climate stability or, conversely, blamed for neglecting the costs of climate change. There are many aspects of capitalism that can be linked to energy efficiency, renewable energy, and adaptation to climate change. The role of capitalism in transcending dysfunctional national politics that are impeding climate policies has some promise for addressing climate issues.[284] The jury is still out, however, on the role of economics and economic models in overcoming the problems of denial ideology. Continued dismissal of the external costs of economic growth as unnecessary distractions will fatally flaw modern industrial societies.

Chapter 4.
Laws, Regulations, and Climate Politics

Ideology drives climate politics more than science does. Denial ideology comes into play when laws and regulations are proposed to address climate change. Politicians use ideology to deny the need for cap and trade, carbon taxes, or EPA regulations. Many of the ideological statements about climate change are expressed as promotion of economic growth and jobs, as we have seen in the previous chapter. Politicians pick up these themes in their statements about climate politics. In this chapter, we will examine three arenas of denial politics: state politics and legislation, national politics, and congressional politics.

State Politics

Koch Industries has funded some of the denial movements discussed in chapter 2 and also has influence in state and local politics. Koch-funded groups such as Americans for Prosperity and the American Legislative Exchange Council (ALEC) are active in state legislatures, where they can have more effect than at the national level. In February 2011, Koch-funded efforts supported a bill to remove New Hampshire from the regional climate initiative. Deputy Majority Leader Shawn Jasper (R-Hudson), who promoted the bill, said, "Neither man nor cow is responsible for global warming." Some of the legislators who voted to sever New Hampshire from RGGI used denial ideology to justify their vote. One said, "The reasons used to promote RGGI were based in false, exaggerated, and highly politicized science."[285] He went on to say, "There is no scientific evidence to support the idea that RGGI does anything to solve this alleged problem."[286] In other words, science is required to validate a specific governmental action such as RGGI. This is an illustration of how politicians confuse the issue, suggesting that scientific "evidence" is required to support a policy, but science does not address such actions directly. Scientific evidence is used to document climate change, but politicians must apply the findings to policies as part of their governance responsibilities.

Although the anti-RGGI bill passed the legislature, Gov. John Lynch vetoed it and the legislature did not override the veto. RGGI has been effective in reducing emissions: "The cap and trade system known as [RGGI] announced on Monday [June 4, 2012] that carbon dioxide emissions from power plants in the nine participating states on the East Coast fell by an average of 23% during the first three years of the program."[287]

Another example of how the denial movement influences politics is a Montana law, proposed by Rep. Joe Read (R), which reads as follows:

An Act Stating Montana's Position on Global Warming

(1) The legislature finds that to ensure economic development in Montana and the appropriate management of Montana's natural resources it is necessary to adopt a public policy regarding global warming.
(2) The legislature finds: (a) Global warming is beneficial to the welfare and business climate of Montana;
(b) Reasonable amounts of carbon dioxide released into the atmosphere have no verifiable impacts on the environment; and
(c) Global warming is a natural occurrence and human activity has not accelerated it.

This legislative language contains a number of denial beliefs: (1) that there is no impact from greenhouse gas emissions; (2) that even if there is some global warming, it is beneficial rather than dangerous;

and (3) that global warming is from natural, not anthropogenic, causes. Legislator Read has elaborated on his rationale for introducing this legislation. In an interview, Read said that "science is driven by grant money" and that "man is very ineffective in instigating that change except in a regional area." [288]

Read uses a number of denial arguments: (1) scientists are doing the research only for money; (2) man is "ineffective" in changing the climate; and (3) even if there is warming, it will be beneficial. While this is a rather extreme example of climate change denial, there are a number of other efforts in state legislatures to prevent the application of climate science to policy. Legislators attempt to repeal the laws of physics with "findings" that deny human influence on the climate, and try to refute the scientific findings on temperature and climate with a legislative fiat. This is an example of how denial ideology overwrites scientific findings by using beliefs to promote dismissal of observations of physical changes.

In 2013, at the time of this writing, Florida, with coastlines and wetlands highly vulnerable to sea-level rise, has a governor who denies climate change and a legislature that has abolished a climate commission. The governor, Rick Scott, said, "I've not been convinced that there's any man-made climate change. Nothing's convinced me that there is." [289] The legislature abolished the Florida Energy and Climate Commission, which had attracted federal funds for energy efficiency.

More general denial proposals inspired by Koch foundations and other denial ideologues are currently under consideration in 22 states. Although they do not explicitly deny climate science, they attempt to accomplish the goal of ending state support for climate science. Eight states have already adopted resolutions asking Congress to block EPA regulations, and 14 other states are considering proposals supported by ALEC (American Legislative Exchange Council), a Koch-funded denial organization of state legislators. The regulations are described as a "train wreck" in the proposals. [290]

The boilerplate proposals are designed to put state legislatures on record as opposing EPA regulations, but only the federal government has the power to directly restrict EPA action. As we will see shortly, there are more direct efforts inspired by the denial movement to restrict EPA regulations through congressional action at the federal level.

ALEC couples an argument that greenhouse gas emissions are not "pollutants" with the demand for a cost-benefit analysis of regulations.[291] This is a popular argument for denial ideologues who seek to deflect concerns about long-term costs and health impacts of climate change with assertions about short-term costs of addressing it. This issue is discussed further under "National Politics" in this chapter.

Renewable portfolio standards are rules adopted by a number of states to increase percentages of renewable energy in generation of electricity. They encourage utilities to build wind farms and adopt other technologies, such as solar thermal, to generate electricity. By opposing these standards, ALEC is undermining the efforts of states to address climate change through its model "Electricity Freedom Act." In proposed legislation, ALEC is trying to get Congress to override state policies by preempting the state standards. As in other cases (see "Congressional Politics" in this chapter), denial ideologues conflate the concept of standards with that of taxes. Renewable portfolio standards are not taxes, and it is possible that adoption of these standards will save money for consumers in the long run. Capital costs for renewable energy are higher than fossil-fueled generation, but operating costs are much lower. The issue of subsidies is not as simplistic as ALEC contends. If existing subsidies for fossil fuels were repealed, prices of electricity generated by the fossil fuels would rise to the level where renewable energy would be competitive. In the United States, subsidies for fossil fuels are more than twice the subsidies for renewable energy.[292] Subsidies cost governments over $500 billion worldwide, and reasonable taxes on fossil fuels could raise another $1.2 trillion for renewable energy infrastructure.[293]

ALEC claims to represent legislators in the states where it has considerable influence. An investigation by the *New York Times* found that corporate board members are the real influence.[294] Many of these corporate board members represent fossil fuel interests, such as Exxon-

Mobil. This raises the question, how representative of the voters are the legislators who toe the ALEC line? State political leaders are often more vulnerable to special interests than national leaders because of the nature of state legislatures—often part-time positions with low pay and little staff support. Legislators can be swayed by ALEC proposals to vote for legislation that may not be in the best interests of their constituents. Corporate sponsorship of ALEC has given companies extraordinary access to legislators, according to Elliott Negin, director of news and commentary at the Union of Concerned Scientists.[295] One of the actions recommended by ALEC is the withdrawal of states from Regional Greenhouse Gas Initiatives (RGGI), based on boilerplate language with blanks to fill in the state's name.[296] The boilerplate proposal was specifically tailored for states in regional climate initiatives. It was introduced in seven states: Michigan, Montana, New Hampshire, New Jersey, New Mexico, Oregon, and Washington. "That model resolution has been quite successful. Arizona, Montana, New Mexico, Oregon, Utah, and Washington quit the Western Climate Initiative, leaving only California and four Canadian provinces."[297]

Sometimes state political leaders turn to religion to provide answers for climate change consequences such as droughts. Texas Gov. Rick Perry called for prayer to relieve his state's drought. Perry's resort to religion to address a scientific issue illustrates denial ideology at work: if the scientific explanations of climate problems cause cognitive dissonance, look for alternative explanations. In a state where fossil fuels have almost a divine status, restrictions on emissions from fossil fuels would be an unacceptable answer. Indeed, Texas has indicated that it will not comply with EPA greenhouse gas regulations.[298] Texas residents continued to rely on divine guidance for adaptation to climate change. Plainfield, Texas, residents formed a prayer group to try to resuscitate a meat-packing plant after severe droughts in 2011 and 2012 decimated cattle herds and led to closing the plant.[299]

It is interesting that political leaders can have faith that a deity can end the effects of climate change, but the same leaders cannot believe in the science that explains the effects. Perhaps because the science is complicated and the scientists project dire consequences, people prefer to believe in more simplistic explanations. I do not mean to be sacrilegious or flippant about the role of prayer in reaction to climate change, but it seems that practical approaches might be more effective.

When he was chairman of the Interstate Oil and Gas Commission, Governor Perry regarded the "radical green energy crowd" as an unscientific elite benefiting from an "avalanche of federal funds."[300] Perry is reflecting the denial ideology argument that climate scientists are greedy for funding and likely to gain from policies designed to restrict fossil fuels. More of Perry's statements on climate change can be found in the section on national politics, below.

Perry's skepticism extends to other Texas officials. When a Rice University professor documented sea-level rises along the coast of Texas, the Texas Commission on Environmental Quality (TCEQ) tried to suppress the report.[301] Texas will probably experience increasing effects of climate change, but apparently the state is not ready to face the music. The article was withdrawn. The sea level continues to rise, however, and it threatens much of the infrastructure of southeast Texas. When politics trumps science, politicians use denial ideology to suppress bad news. They try to hide problems for which they have no solutions. Although Texas politicians may, like King Canute, try to hold back the tide, they will eventually have to deal with sea-level consequences of climate change.

Another state with a denial approach to sea level is North Carolina. House Bill 819 proposes to exclude anything about sea-level rise other than a linear extrapolation of historical data: "The Division of Coastal Management shall be the only State agency authorized to develop rates of sea-level rise and shall do so only at the request of the Commission. **These rates shall only be determined using historical data, and these data shall be limited to the time period following the year 1900. Rates of sea-level rise may be extrapolated linearly to estimate future rates of rise but shall not include scenarios of accelerated**

rates of sea-level rise."[302] In other words, the commission can veto any scenario that projects a higher rate of sea-level rise than the average rate of the 20th century. If the 21st century starts showing a higher rate of rise, that evidence must be ignored in favor of a belief that the past rate is the only one possible—the essence of denial ideology.

By legislative fiat, the North Carolina General Assembly is excluding any projection that is not a linear extrapolation of historical data. In other words, projections by scientists that sea-level rise may accelerate due to global warming are denied by fiat, as if the General Assembly could hold back the tide. Of course, coastal real estate values and property taxes are threatened by climate change, so it is better to deny reality and hope nothing happens. Fear of reality drives politicians to do strange things.

Just to make sure that state agencies and local jurisdictions do not thwart the will of the General Assembly, a bill was introduced to prohibit them from enacting greenhouse gas regulations. The purpose of the bill was stated as follows:

> AN ACT TO PROHIBIT STATE AGENCIES AND LO-
> CAL GOVERNMENTS FROM ADOPTING, IMPLE-
> MENTING, OR ENFORCING A RULE OR ORDI-
> NANCE THAT REGULATES GREENHOUSE GAS
> EMISSIONS OR LIMITS HUMAN ACTIVITY FOR
> THE PURPOSE OF REDUCING GREENHOUSE GAS
> EMISSIONS IF THE RULE OR ORDINANCE IS NOT
> REQUIRED BY A FEDERAL REGULATION OR LAW
> OR IS MORE STRINGENT THAN A CORRESPOND-
> ING FEDERAL REGULATION OR LAW.[303]

While state governments deny that climate change causes sea-level rise, local governments have to deal with the consequences. Virginia, whose attorney general has tried to use the state's power to suppress climate science (see below), has problems with sea-level rise. Nearly 10% of Norfolk neighborhoods are subject to storm surges. The real consequences of climate change are beginning to impact people's lives in direct, costly ways. Adaptation to climate change will loom ever larger since politicians are unwilling to address mitigation through regulation of fossil fuel emissions. The Virginia state legislature is considering a bill to aid Norfolk and other coastal cities, but the bill's sponsors are unwilling to use the term "sea-level rise" because it implies that climate science is valid. Instead, they use the term "recurrent flooding."[304] Whatever the terminology, it is obvious that Virginia is going to face the consequences of climate change in the near future.

Many states have enacted or proposed specific actions that reflect denial ideology. One of the most direct denial actions is that of Utah.[305] Utah's legislature wants the EPA to deny the Supreme Court mandate that requires the endangerment finding (i.e., the finding that climate change endangers public health). It bases this proposal on canards such as "global temperatures have been level and declining in some areas over the past 12 years." It labels climate scientists as "alarmists" who are manipulating the science. The resolution incorporates canards about declining temperatures and the inability of models to account for recent changes. Utah's proposed resolution evoked the following comment from an observer: "Utah's official stance on climate change is that it does not exist. Presumably, there is a vast liberal conspiracy propagating the rumor that Earth is warming due to carbon emissions. So the Utah legislature is filled with idiots."[306]

While I would not go as far as to call legislators "idiots," it is clear many are uninformed or misinformed, particularly about the "vast liberal conspiracy propagating the rumor that Earth is warming." Clearly, these legislators do not know climate science. Or if they are well informed, they may still bow to pressure from denial ideologues and mandate "teaching the controversy."

A peculiar example of state politics in action with regard to climate science is the State of Virginia's suit against the University of Virginia. Michael Mann, the scientist whose work on the "hockey stick" is described in chapter 1, did some of his research at UVa. The state attorney general, Ken Cuccinelli, sued UVa to obtain records of the research and Mann's e-mails, some of which were included in the "Climategate" scandal described in chapter 1. He cited the Virginia Fraud against Taxpayers Act.[307]

Academic freedom is necessary to defend scientific research. If political interests distort science, it may be less valid; in the case of climate science, this is a highly fraught risk because of the intensity of political polarization. Conservative politicians in Virginia are attacking not only climate science but also the general principle of the independence of science from politics. However, Cuccinelli lost his case in the Virginia Supreme Court, and Mann responded: "It's sad, though, that so much money and resources had to be wasted on Cuccinelli's witch hunt against me and the University of Virginia, when it could have been invested, for example, in measures to protect Virginia's coastline from the damaging effects of sea-level rise it is already seeing."[308]

Mann's response goes to the heart of climate change issues: whether to spend money on denial or adaptation/mitigation. Because so much political capital (and taxpayer money) is diverted to denial, some basic climate actions are neglected. Unless politicians demur from attacking science, policies will continue to represent ideology.

Another peculiar example of state politics involving climate change is the action by several states to distort the teaching of climate science. Sometimes this seems as innocuous as postulating that climate science is a "theory" in contrast to other "theories" such as denial. "In…South Dakota, the state House has already passed a resolution saying climate change should be taught as a theory rather than a proven fact."[309] The text of that resolution reads as follows:

> The South Dakota Legislature urges that instruction in the public schools relating to global warming include the following: (1) That global warming is a scientific theory rather than a proven fact; (2) That there are a variety of climatological, meteorological, astrological, thermological, cosmological, and ecological dynamics

that can effect [sic] world weather phenomena and that the significance and interrelativity of these factors is largely speculative; (3) That the debate on global warming has subsumed political and philosophical viewpoints which have complicated and prejudiced the scientific investigation of global warming phenomena.

South Dakota legislators apparently have a supernatural approach to climate science. They invoke astrology to explain weather phenomena. It is not a coincidence that this belief system would appear in a resolution based on ideology, as ideology itself is sometimes based on supernatural premises. It is also no coincidence that the resolution uses terms such as "political and philosophical viewpoints," since the resolution itself is a political statement.

Oklahoma's proposed law seems rather innocuous. It seems to confirm the concepts of "critical thinking, logical analysis, open and objective discussion of scientific theories," but it opens the door to denial ideology:

> The State Board of Education, upon the request of a school district board of education, shall allow and assist teachers, principals, and school administrators in creating an environment within the public school system that promotes critical thinking, logical analysis, open and objective discussion of scientific theories, including, but not limited to, evolution, the origin of life, global warming, and human cloning. Assistance shall include support and guidance for teachers regarding effective ways to help students understand, analyze, critique, and objectively review scientific theories being studied, including those enumerated in this subsection.[310]

While the language sounds reasonable enough, the intent of the legislation is to allow teachers to teach denial ideology alongside climate science. This is the equivalent of teaching creationism alongside biology. Another bill was introduced to add language for teaching the controversy:

> The Legislature further finds that the teaching of some scientific concepts, including but not limited to premises in the areas of biology, chemistry, meteorology, bioethics, and physics, can cause controversy, and that some teachers may be unsure of the expectations concerning how they should present information on some subjects, such as, but not limited to, biological evolution, the chemical origins of life, global warming, and human cloning.[311]

The State Board of Education and the school district boards are likely to find plenty of material to introduce denial ideology as a counterargument to global warming. Providing this material to students as a means of "balancing" climate science does them a disservice. It will provide the next generation with a rationalization to doubt the information (see the preface) that they will need to live in a changed world. The "balance" is between science, which is testable, and ideology, which is not. They are not comparable and thus are different world views.

Another state that has taken up the cause of "balanced" science education is Louisiana. Its proposed law promotes: "An environment within public elementary and secondary schools that promotes critical thinking skills, logical analysis, and open and objective discussion of scientific theories being studied including…global warming." The bill also calls for "instructional materials to help students understand, analyze, critique, and review scientific theories in an objective manner."

Many of these state proposals and resolutions stem from the work of ALEC, the American Legislative Exchange Council, discussed earlier in this chapter. Although these actions are mostly resolutions and proposals, they show a trend by state legislators to build denial ideology into state educational systems. "Teaching the controversy" has been a favorite tactic of denial ideologues, and these proposals institutionalize it. An example is the law that passed in Tennessee. There, the legislature seems to think that climate science raises "controversial issues." To assert this is a misreading of the science as advocacy, which it is not. The Tennessee bill was passed over objections by a list of scientific bodies: the National Association of Biology Teachers, the American Association for the Advancement of Science, the American Civil Liberties Union of Tennessee, the American Institute for Biological Sciences, the Knoxville *News Sentinel*, the Nashville *Tennessean*, the National Association of Geoscience Teachers, the National Earth Science Teachers Association, the Tennessee Science Teachers Association, and all eight Tennessee members of the National Academy of Sciences. These organizations are on the front lines of science education and have to deal with the political pressures stimulated by denial ideology.

Scientific data are measurable but not bifurcated into "either-or" propositions. Teachers can present climate science as a scientific explanation, but presenting denial as a counterproposition is to move the discussion from a scientific plane to an ideological level. Scientific explanations are subject to revision as more information becomes available; ideological positions are rarely revised.

The National Center for Science Education (NCSE) has also reacted to these tactics in state legislatures. Its director linked the "controversy" over climate science to the earlier one over teaching evolution. NCSE has also noted that an effect of denial ideology is that climate science is not even included in the science curriculum of public schools, or, if it is taught, the "debate" is also included. Pressure from parents or even other teachers to avoid the subject is probably generated from denial groups such as the Tea Party or Americans for Prosperity. Like the groups who keep surveillance on science teachers who teach evolution, these groups probably receive reports from parents of students and from other teachers. They then come back at the science teachers or school administrators with requests to "teach the controversy" or not teach climate science at all.[312]

The effect of denial ideology on teachers is devastating. They are subject to strong pressures to stop teaching science, or "teach the controversy." These pressures can be particularly acute when teachers use resources such as films on climate change.[313] *An Inconvenient Truth*, the Oscar-winning film by Al Gore, has drawn a lot of resistance from denial advocates. Often this is expressed at the state and local levels, where teachers and others can be attacked for essentially doing their job. Climate science seems to draw even more ire than teaching evolution and sex education. As a result of these attacks, teachers have become reticent about teaching climate science, and American education is becoming deficient in science.[314]

On the more general issue of science education, observers have noted a general tendency to "dumb down" American education.[315] One of the real dangers of "dumbing down" the electorate is that scientific illiteracy threatens democratic decision making. Lack of understanding of climate science by the electorate will result, and has resulted in these states, in uninformed decisions about climate change. As one observer notes, powerful interests can corrupt the process, and the Koch brothers certainly have exerted power through ALEC.[316]

One last example of denial in state politics is provided by Ken Cuccinelli, attorney general of the State of Virginia, who ran for governor in the 2013 election with the support of many petroleum interests. He sued the University of Virginia to obtain records on Michael Mann, as described in above, but lost the case. He has also sued the EPA to stop greenhouse gas regulations. Speaking at a Tea Party rally, Cuccinelli said, "The attorney general's office is a very reactive office. We wouldn't be suing the EPA if the EPA did not abandon all semblance of science and law to put out its endangerment finding on the CO_2. Now, let's make them all happy just for a moment and everybody just hold your breath." Cuccinelli paused several seconds before saying. "There you go, just a short period of time with no CO_2. Now the trees are going to protest, but at least the EPA will be happy."[317] The absurdity of his statement was apparently lost on the candidate.

Of course, this recital of state politics would be incomplete without mention of a number of states that are, in fact, pursuing policies to mitigate emissions. California is taking the lead, as it has with other aspects of air pollution. AB 32 is a state law that establishes GHG emission caps, and the state is designing policies to implement a cap and trade system. The law has withstood both referendum and lawsuit opposition.

It remains to be seen if AB 32 is successful in reducing emissions. It has drawn a lot of resistance from denial advocates and others who contend that the costs will be unbearable, but the state's experience with the law will test those contentions. Other Western states have followed California's lead. In the Northeast, there is the Regional Greenhouse Gas Initiative (RGGI), mentioned previously. New England and other Northeast states, including New York, Maryland, and Delaware, are members. New Jersey recently dropped out.

These state initiatives are both beneficial and harmful to national politics. The benefit is that the states are trying various approaches that can become models for national policies if they pan out. The harm, from the viewpoint of business, is that there is now a patchwork of policies that may become costly to implement in different ways. Of course, with California taking the lead, most businesses tend to adjust to California's standards when planning national marketing strategies.

National Politics

Politicians in the 2012 presidential election campaigns adopted denial ideology. Several, including Newt Gingrich, Tim Pawlenty, and Mitt Romney, had previously expressed support for policies to mitigate climate change but changed their tunes when confronted by a primary season overlaid by denial ideology. Others, including Michelle Bachman, Ron Paul, Rick Perry, and Rick Santorum, maintained denial positions throughout the campaign. A few examples will illustrate this difference.

Michelle Bachman was a sponsor of legislation to repeal efficiency standards, which she justified with a statement about the "global warming hoax."[318] She described climate polices as follows: "Carbon dioxide is natural, it is not harmful. It is part of Earth's life cycle, and yet we're being told that we have to reduce this natural substance, reduce the American standard of living, to create an arbitrary reduction in something that is naturally occurring in Earth."[319] Bachmann seems to be, like Governor Perry, a believer in the divine origin of natural disasters. "I don't know how much God has to do to get the attention of the politicians. We've had an earthquake; we've had a hurricane. He said, 'Are you going to start listening to me here?' "[320]

Bachmann's coupling of earthquakes and hurricanes mixed metaphors of "acts of God." While an earthquake might be an act of God from the viewpoint of divine retribution, the hurricane had a boost from man in the form of warm seas. Nevertheless, the idea that natural disasters are purely acts of God, not man, is a denial talking point.

Ron Paul called global warming "the greatest hoax I think that has been around for many years."[321]

Rick Perry was one of the strongest denial ideologues among Republican candidates. Perry said climate science is "all one contrived, phony mess that is falling apart under its own weight."[322] As we have seen in the discussion of state politics, Governor Perry regarded consequences of climate change, such as droughts, as "acts of God" best addressed through prayer. Candidate Perry also prayed for a change in national policies.[323] Perry, like other presidential candidates, wrote a book in which he attacked EPA regulations.[324] In his book, Perry used an argument that often appears in denial ideology—that regulation of carbon emissions is not authorized by legislation and would have "devastating" economic effects. His argument is not supported by legal history (see below) or by many business leaders (chapter 5). Perry also used denial ideology to attack Democrats. He asserted that "science gets hijacked by the political Left" and "may not stand the test of time."[325] He repeated the canard about a cooling trend to suggest that climate science is invalid. He then extended this argument to accuse scientists of manipulating data for their own benefit: "There are a substantial number of scientists who have manipulated data so that they would have dollars rolling in to their projects."[326]

Perry also adopted the strategy developed by Luntz and Milloy (see below), using doubt and "controversy" about climate science to reject its findings. "I don't think from my perspective that I want America to be engaged in spending that much money on [what is] still a scientific theory that has not been proven and from my perspective is more and more being put into question," he said in New Hampshire.[327] His assertion that the "scientific theory" of climate science is "more and more being put into question" reflected arguments by denial ideologues that there is widespread uncertainty and debate among climate scientists. While tendentious, this argument gained traction among the voting public, according to surveys (see below). Perry accused scientists of manipulating data, another denial argument.[328] This argument draws on supposed evidence from "Climategate," the East Anglia University climate unit's e-mail that purportedly identified incidents of data manipulation. As noted above, these accusations have been disproved and have had no effect on the basic science. Nevertheless, politicians will continue to "teach the controversy" to avoid confronting the facts of climate science that might undermine their energy policies.

Perry's position on climate change, which may not be consonant with the findings of climate science, is nevertheless compatible with many voters'. As observed by Clayton Morris, a commentator for Fox News: "If you dive into the weeds a little bit on this global warming thing, you see that it seems that facts are certainly on [presidential candidate Jon] Huntsman's side on all of this and fact checkers have come out, we're actually having our own brain room look at this right now, that any of Perry's comments don't seem to hold a lot of water. It doesn't matter. What's resonating right now in South Carolina is helping Governor Perry tremendously, and he fired back at Huntsman on global warming and [is] gaining traction, facts or not."[329] This was a remarkable admission by Fox News, which generally promotes denial ideology. The conservative press not only promotes denial, but also exults in the fact that denial ideology has "traction" among voters despite its invalidity.

In a candidates' debate in September 2011, Perry compared climate skeptics to Galileo, who was attacked by the established religion of his time. Ironically, the scientists whom Perry is defending, for example, Roy Spencer and Fred Singer, are affiliated with religious conservatives. Spencer is affiliated with the Cornwall Alliance (described previously), and Singer is affiliated with the Moonies, the Unification Church, founded by Rev. Sun Myung Moon. A more apt comparison to Galileo might be James Hansen, who has been persecuted for his writings and testimony about the imminent dangers of climate change. Denial ideology in Galileo's time defended the unscientific view that the sun revolves around the earth; denial ideology today downplays the science of climate change.

Perry was challenged on his position but remained adamant that climate change is not an "incontrovertible" scientific finding. He echoed the position of Norwegian physicist Ivar Giaever, who says, " 'Incontrovertible' is not a scientific word. Nothing is incontrovertible in science."[330] In a superficial way, Giaever and Perry were correct. Science is never a closed intellectual system, if that is what they mean by "incontrovertible." Scientific findings are always open to challenge and correction. Climate science has been challenged many times and continues to provide evidence of climate change. Corrections are welcomed. But to ignore the evidence because of a philosophical difference is to jeopardize future generations.

Rick Santorum said that climate change is "a beautifully concocted scheme [that is] just an excuse for more government control of your life."[331] He contended that "there is no such thing as global warming... It's just an excuse for more government control of your life, and I've never been for any scheme or even accepted the junk science behind the whole narrative."[332] Santorum apparently subscribed to the denial argument that climate science is "junk science," a common phrase in denial ideology.[333] With regard to the Keystone Pipeline, opposed by environmentalists because of its contribution to global warming,

Santorum also indicated a disdain for environmentalists. Like many denial advocates, Santorum saw climate science as "a religion of its own that's being pushed on the American public."[334] It is ironic, coming from a candidate who prides himself on his religious credentials, that science is just another "religion." He confuses ideology and religion without regard for the essential difference of empirical versus nonempirical phenomena. To confuse religion, which is nonempirical, with ideology, which is empirical, can create serious errors of judgment and policy. Santorum repeats the Cornwall Alliance argument that CO_2 emissions are so minuscule that they could have no effect on climate.[335] This canard might appeal to those already predisposed to denial by belittling the effect of greenhouse gas emissions on the climate. It is clear that the denial argument Santorum uses is not subject to scientific proof or disproof. By calling CO_2 emissions a "minor factor of a minor factor," he tries to deny their effect.

Santorum accused climate scientists of being "sentimental" and "radical" and says they are plotting to "take over the fossil fuel industry."[336] He also uses phrases such as the "politicization of science called man-made warming,"[337] which is an ironic description of what Santorum himself is doing. But the use of terms like "radical" and "sentimental" indicates Santorum is polarizing the issue and resting his argument on untestable beliefs. Santorum also repeated the denial argument that environmentalists are using climate science as a means of controlling society and the economy.[338] Santorum displayed the kind of thinking that appeals to denial followers: "supporters of climate policies" are trying to take over "allocation of resources" so that they can "force you to do what you should do" in economic and social decisions.[339] This argument makes one major assumption: that policies to address climate change are going to be unnecessary because there will be no global warming. But if natural processes force societies to adapt, environmentalists will not determine allocation of resources. Policies and allocation of resources will be carried out by a desperate government forced to respond to crises exacerbated by delayed action on climate change.

Among the candidates that changed positions were Newt Gingrich, Tim Pawlenty, and Mitt Romney.

Pawlenty, former governor of Minnesota, called his previous position on climate change a "mistake."[340] Pawlenty has waffled on the key question of climate science, how much humans contribute to climate change.[341] After indicating some confusion on the issue of climate change, Pawlenty switched gears and talked about a "government, top-down scheme" as if the science dictates that approach. While it is normal for politicians to waffle and change their views, the need to apologize and reverse course indicates that pressure from the denial movements, especially the Tea Party, colored the views of candidates. They realize that it is probably unsustainable to deny climate science, but they shy away from discussing its implications for energy policy.

In 2007, before he became a candidate for president, Newt Gingrich made a public-interest announcement, along with former House Speaker Nancy Pelosi, supporting policies to curb emissions. Now, Gingrich rejects his previous support for cap and trade. "Gingrich doesn't think climate science supports the need for policies to curb emissions."[342] Republican candidates had to play to a Tea Party base to have any chance for nomination. Gingrich displayed this tendency in a number of statements he made.[343] One of the most egregious was that no "threat from global warming is big enough to justify destroying the American economy."[344] Many have argued the exact opposite, that not addressing global warming would destroy the American economy.

Romney, as governor of Massachusetts, supported cap-and-trade policies for power plant emissions: "This is a great thing for the Commonwealth (of Massachusetts). We can effectively create incentives to help stimulate a sector of the economy and at the same time not kill jobs."[345] He said that "Massachusetts continues to be committed to improving air quality for all our citizens. These carbon emission limits will provide real and immediate progress in the battle to improve our environment."[346]

During his acceptance speech at the Republican National Convention in August 2012, Romney chided President Obama: "President Obama promised to slow the rise of the oceans and to heal the planet. My promise…is to help you and your family."

Left unsaid was the effect of rising oceans on storm surges, such as those that occurred in 2012 as Romney was making his speech when Hurricane Isaac was flooding many parts of the coasts of Mississippi and Louisiana. How did Romney help those people? Perhaps he should have listened to one of his own party members, who told a reporter: "We've just got to get better on conservation issues, especially climate change, if we want to remain the majority party."[347] Nevertheless, Romney told a reporter that there "remains a lack of scientific consensus on the issue— on the extent of the warming, the extent of the human contribution, and the severity of the risk."[348]

Romney tended to waffle on climate science: "He believes the climate is changing but he does not know the extent to which human activity is contributing to it."[349] He questions one of the key tenets of climate science, that carbon dioxide is a pollutant.[350] Because the EPA has designated CO2 as a pollutant under the Clean Air Act and used this definition for an "endangerment finding," Romney retorts: "I don't think that was the intent of the original legislation, and I don't think carbon is a pollutant in the sense of harming our bodies."[351]

Romney's point about "not harming our bodies" is an issue that has plagued climate science. How can scientists equate carbon dioxide, which is ubiquitous and harmless in low concentrations (presently 400 parts per million), with poisons such as sulfur dioxide that can kill fish and trees, or nitrous oxide that can cause asthma? Scientists do not in fact equate the different pollutants, but instead analyze each separately. The effects of CO2 are long-term effects that increase over time and will affect health increasingly through droughts, floods, extreme weather, and shifts in the climate zones of pests. Heat waves can also be deadly, as many in Europe discovered in 2003 and many in the United States in 2011. Denial that CO2 is a pollutant is semantic sleight of hand, an attempt to define away the problem. This is not scientifically valid, although some denial advocates may believe it is legalistically valid and politically popular.

Romney's website for the 2012 presidential campaign also repeated the canard that CO2 is not a pollutant. He recommended that Congress "amend [the] Clean Air Act to exclude carbon dioxide from its purview."[352] One could argue that this statement recognizes that CO2 is now in the purview of the Clean Air Act, so that it requires amendment to exclude it. In fact, if one examines the definitions in the act, CO2 is not specifically mentioned, but it does cover "any physical, chemical… substance or matter which is emitted or otherwise enters the ambient air." CO2 would have to be specifically excluded from the act, an absurd exemption to the scientific definition of air pollutant. The actual text of the Clean Air Act, US Code Title 42, Chapter 85, Subchapter III, § 7602, defines pollutant so broadly that it can include carbon dioxide:

(g) The term "air pollutant" means any air pollution agent or combination of such agents, including any physical, chemical, biological, radioactive (including source material, special nuclear material, and byproduct material) substance or matter which is emitted into or otherwise enters the ambient air. Such term includes any precursors to the formation of any air pollutant, to the extent the Administrator has identified such precursor or precursors for the particular purpose for which the term "air pollutant" is used. (h) All language referring to effects on welfare includes, but is not limited to, effects on soils, water, crops, vegetation, manmade materials, animals, wildlife, weather, visibility, and *climate*, damage to and deterioration of property, and hazards to transportation, as well as effects on economic values and on personal comfort and well-being, whether caused by transformation, conversion, or combination with other air pollutants." (Emphasis added.)

The law specifically mentions climate and defines *pollutant* in a way that can be applied to carbon dioxide, methane, and other greenhouse gases. The US Supreme Court has mandated that the EPA include carbon dioxide as a pollutant under this definition. It based this on the principle that carbon dioxide at higher concentrations than natural levels can create an endangerment to health and welfare through climate change. This "endangerment" finding is one of the main points of conflict among politicians and ideologues.

Romney's campaign counted on public support for his position that CO2 is not a pollutant, but recent polling indicates that this was risky. Even two-thirds of the Republican "base" agreed that CO2 is a pollutant.[353] In other words, the public supported not only the Clean Air Act pollution standards, but also precisely the definition of carbon dioxide as a pollutant. Courts have also confirmed that CO2 is a pollutant requiring EPA regulation.[354]

One should carefully analyze politicians' statements to determine the degree to which they are based on denial ideology. Not all opposition to policies such as EPA regulations or regional greenhouse gas initiatives was based solely on denial ideology. To varying degrees, politicians and their supporters subscribe to the ideology for expedient as well as philosophical reasons, and politicians accept some conclusions of climate science while opposing specific policies. But the overall effect of denial ideology has been clear: there are few effective climate policies in the United States, mainly at the local and state levels, and strong opposition stymies national policy.

Much of the denial ideology relies on the raising of doubt by contrarians, who may have some scientific credentials but do not specialize in scientific research on climate.[355] A master at the creation of doubt was Frank Luntz, a media consultant for Republican candidates. In a 2003 memo, Luntz stated: "The Scientific Debate Remains Open. Voters believe that there is no consensus about global warming within the scientific community. Should the public come to believe that the scientific issues are settled, their views about global warming will change accordingly. Therefore, you need to make the lack of scientific certainty a primary issue in the debate, and defer to scientists and other experts in the field."[356]

For the 2012 election, political advisor Steven Milloy offered similar advice in an op-ed piece in the *Washington Times* titled "2012 GOP guide to the climate debate: Candidates need to be ready to blow away the arguments." He said, "We don't agree, however, that man-made emissions of carbon dioxide (CO_2) and other greenhouse gases are having either detectable or predictable effects on climate...According to climate alarmists, this should have caused measurable global warming. But none has been observed, a fact that finally was admitted by climate alarmists in the wake of the Climategate scandal."[357]

Milloy's argument was specious; as we have seen, it has already been refuted by the NOAA data cited previously.[358] The NOAA data show that 2000–2010 was the warmest decade on record and temperatures exceeded the average for the 1990s. Further, there has been no admission by "climate alarmists" that temperatures have stabilized, despite the extraneous reference to Climategate. The only purpose of citing Climategate is to suggest that climate science is controversial. Use of the term "alarmists," pervasive in denial ideology, is strange. It would be more accurate to call those who say that the US economy would be ruined by climate policies "alarmists." The resilience of the economy and innovation in energy technology would put the lie to these critics.[359]

By framing the discussion of climate science as controversial, denial ideologues sometimes succeeded in convincing journalists and others to give as much weight to the denial of climate science as its affirmation. This serves the purposes of those who want to raise doubts about the science and delay action. The "controversy" strategy has succeeded to a remarkable degree. When asked in a 2010 poll, slightly more than half of respondents believed that there is a lot of disagreement among scientists than said that scientists agree that global warming is happening.[360] In fact, 97% of scientists agree. Public opinion, based on misinformation about climate science, is due to the work of the denial ideologues, who consider it useful to keep the public misinformed on the science.

It is clear that the 2012 election had enormous significance for climate change. Scientists have identified the next decade as crucial for controlling greenhouse gas emissions. "Global emissions must peak between 2015 and 2017. That means the next presidential administration will be the most important one there will ever be when it comes to overcoming global warming, making this the most consequential presidential election ever on climate change."[361] If candidates are unwilling to acknowledge this challenge, the opportunities for lower-cost, effective measures will diminish rapidly. Delay in implementing policies will be much more costly later.[362]

Barack Obama, who won the 2012 presidential election but faces a hostile Congress, has made clear his stance on climate change. While not making it as high a priority as health care in his first two years in office, he endorsed the regulatory approach of the EPA. In his 2013 inaugural speech, Obama criticized climate change denial: "Some may still deny the overwhelming judgment of science, but none can avoid the devastating impact of raging fires and crippling drought and more powerful storms."[363] With regard to his reelection, "The President has said that the most important policy he could address in his second term is climate change, one of the few issues that he thinks could fundamentally improve the world decades from now."[364]

Obama attacked Republicans during 2012 for denial positions. "You've got a party that denies climate change even exists, rather than debates how to address it," he noted.[365] After one Republican debate, he said, "I mean, has anybody been watching the debates lately? You've got a governor whose state is on fire denying climate change."[366]

The staff of Texas governor Perry responded in kind: "It's outrageous President Obama would use the burning of 1,500 homes, the worst fires in state history, as a political attack," said Perry spokesman Ray Sullivan. "This from a president whose nation is financially suffering and his solution is taking more money away from families by raising taxes on families and small businesses."[367]

Obama's position on regulation drew the ire of denial ideologues. Sen. James Inhofe (R-OK) stated the denial position most baldly:

> Even though global warming hysteria and cap and trade are long dead, the fight is far from over because President

Obama is now moving forward with a plan to achieve through regulation what could not be achieved through legislation. In December of 2009, the Obama EPA issued what is called the "endangerment finding"—a finding that greenhouse gases harm public health and welfare. Armed with this "finding," the EPA is planning to regulate greenhouse gases instead through the Clean Air Act, which was never meant to regulate carbon. Like cap and trade, this plan will have the same $300 [billion]–$400 billion price tag, it will put the same amount of jobs in jeopardy, and it will cause the same amount of havoc for our economy. My fight today is to stop them from achieving this cap and trade agenda through the back door.[368]

Inhofe touched a number of bases in the denial movement that make him one of its leading ideologues. He used "hysteria" to describe climate science, pronounced cap and trade dead (tell that to California), attacked the "endangerment" finding, and exaggerated the costs to the economy and jobs. All of these have been refuted (see chapters 1, 3, and 5). He misstated the authority of the Clean Air Act, which, as noted above, has legal authority to regulate greenhouse gases. His pet peeves are standard canards of the denial movement and the basis of polarization of climate policy. He tried to get the Senate to endorse his positions by offering an amendment to a budget bill that "stops the EPA from having the jurisdiction over the regulation of carbon" by defunding the agency's greenhouse gas regulations. It was defeated by a vote of 52 to 47.

Senator Inhofe represents a state that has suffered from a number of extreme weather events. A fellow senator, Sheldon Whitehouse (D-RI), noted that states represented by Inhofe and others tend to be the ones that climate change affects the most. "I'll tell you why. We're stuck in this together. We are stuck in this together. When cyclones tear up Oklahoma and hurricanes swamp Alabama and wildfires scorch Texas, you come to us, the rest of the country, for billions of dollars to recover.

And the damage that your polluters and deniers are doing doesn't just hit Oklahoma and Alabama and Texas. It hits Rhode Island with floods and storms. It hits Oregon with acidified seas. It hits Montana with dying forests. So, like it or not, we're in this together."[369] Whitehouse's statement demonstrates the widespread effect of denial: even when the politicians who represent affected areas continue to deny the cause of extreme weather, they incur costs for everyone.

It will be difficult to overcome the effects of denial ideology. A recent case in point: the Solyndra loan from the Energy Department went sour when the company declared bankruptcy. Republican members of the Energy and Commerce subcommittee on oversight and investigations pounced on the case and declared that the Obama administration was trying to "pick winners." When politicians deny climate science, they also deny the need for action to deal with the consequences of climate science. This creates a wide gap in understanding the future and raises questions about humanity's ability to manage the unavoidable and avoid the unmanageable.

Even worse, the misuse of science by denial ideologues corrupts the political communication process. Erosion of the integrity of science by denial of its findings is a highly corrosive effect of denial ideology.[370] Because of this type of partisanship, climate policy has become gridlocked at the national level. This polarization tends to delay effective action and leads to desperation when the effects of climate change become much more difficult to manage.[371]

Polarization

Why has climate change become a polarizing issue? According to a poll by the Public Religion Research Institute (PRRI), Republicans have split evenly on the issue.[372] In other words, polarization on climate change may be a result of campaigning in which the Republican candidates appeal to their base by denying climate change. More moderate Republicans may not turn out for primary elections to the same degree as the base. As a result, Republican members of Congress are not representative of Republican voters when the members deny climate change. This interpretation was confirmed by McCright and Dunlap, who suggested climate had joined abortion and other issues as a mainstay of America's hardening Left-Right gap and stated, "The culture wars have thus taken on a new dimension."[373] Hamilton also confirms this analysis, stating that climate denial "has now become a marker of cultural identity in the 'angry' parts of the United States."[374]

When an issue such as climate change transitions from a scientific to a cultural issue, it becomes intractable and denial loses its anchorage in rational thought. It also makes action on climate change much more difficult: "In Washington, 'climate change' has become a lightning rod; it's a four-letter word," said Andrew J. Hoffman, director of the University of Michigan's Erb Institute for Sustainable Development.[375] The denial movement reinforces the cultural conflict by assigning nefarious motivation to the scientists whose findings seem to threaten the lifestyles of the denial movement members.

Polarization is dysfunctional for formulation of policies in a democracy. "As many commentators have warned, the growth of ideologically polarized politics may prove toxic to government effectiveness and perhaps even to America's social stability."[376] It has this effect because the compromises necessary to resolve issues of energy and climate change become more and more remote as the issues become further polarized.

Polarization also has a way of reinforcing denial tendencies, even among people who are not predisposed to deny climate science.[377] When "skepticism" makes climate change a political issue rather than an informational issue, denial ideology has an advantage. It provides people with an excuse to ignore signs of climate change and tune out climate science. This skepticism is generated entirely by denial ideology with its false assertions about reality.

Polarization is fueled by corporate money that has increased exponentially since the Citizens United decision by the Supreme Court in 2011. One observer related that decision to denial advocacy.[378] Polarization of climate politics has a dampening effect on climate policies. When the EPA is caught up in climate politics, its actions are delayed and reduced in effectiveness. Its rules regarding emissions from power plants and refineries are subjected to legal and political challenges.

As we have seen throughout the discussion of national politics, the effect of the politicians' denial statements is to make climate science a political football. Rather than confronting the consequences of climate change and educating voters about policies to resolve the issue, politicians tend to make it a "win-lose" proposition. If denial advocates win, the earth loses.

Congressional Politics

If presidential politics polarizes the issue, congressional politics is even more polarizing. The House of Representatives was highly polarized and unrepresentative of 2012 voters, 51% of whom voted for Democrats.[379] Republican "representatives" are not representative of the majority of American people on climate change issues. More than half of Republican members of the House and 65% of Republican senators deny human-caused climate change; more than 90% of the Republican leadership of both houses deny it.[380] They do not even represent Republican voters. "Only 35% of the Republican respondents said they agree with the Republican Party's position on climate change."[381] Most Republican voters support action on climate change: "62% favor taking action to combat climate change, such as taxing carbon pollution."[382]

Denial congressmen are not independent thinkers who can decide on issues on their merits, but a group of politicians intimidated by opponents in primary elections and interest groups who fund their campaigns. They are beholden to the Tea Party, Americans for Prosperity, and other interest groups who deny climate change.

Congress reflects the polarization of interest groups in society. Many interest groups pressure Congress to favor their special interests in contrast to the public interest. When those interests coincide with the denial ideology, they reinforce polarization. Republican members have often attacked the EPA for drafting emissions regulations. Blaming regulations for outsourcing jobs is a common argument among followers of denial movements. It combines the ideology of unrestricted growth as necessary to maintain "Americans' standard of living" with the denial argument that there is "no environmental benefit" to regulating greenhouse gas emissions.

In the case of congressional politics involving climate change, the main pressure comes from fossil fuel interests. These fossil fuel organizations invoke market justifications for opposing restrictions on greenhouse gas emissions.[383] Coal and oil executives do not necessarily reflect the views of all business leaders, however. Indeed, utilities, the main customers of coal companies, sometimes disagree with coal executives and with the members of Congress who represent coal interests.[384] One former CEO of West Virginia utilities said, "If you're a West Virginian and a coal company and you're denying climate change, it's sort of like denying you've got cancer and hoping it will get better. It won't. And the longer you deny it, the worse the fall will be."[385] Since the main consumers of coal, electric utilities, are not unanimously opposed to regulations, denial advocates turn to other rationales to justify their opposition. This opposition came to a head in the House of Representatives with the introduction by Representative Fred Upton (R-MI) of the "Energy Tax Prevention Act," aimed at preventing the EPA from enforcing climate change regulations. Upton is chairman of the House Committee on Energy and Commerce, which overseas EPA regulations. As we have already seen, his justification for preventing EPA action is jobs, jobs, and jobs.

Representative Upton stated, in his hearings about EPA regulations: "We live in a global economy with global competition, and nations like China have absolutely no intention of similarly burdening their interests...Manufacturing jobs will leave this country unless [the] EPA is stopped."[386] He also disputed the EPA endangerment finding, which is based on threats to air quality and health.

Upton commits one major error in describing cap and trade as "cap and tax," a common misstatement by denial advocates. No taxes are contemplated, but the term is a red flag for many denial movement members. This is ironic, because cap and trade is a conservative concept; Republicans introduced it and George H. W. Bush endorsed it. Douglas Holt-Eakin, former adviser to George W. Bush, said, "There's a conservative principle that says government can do good by intervening with appropriate regulations, like cap and trade. It's gotten to be such a loaded word in Washington you can't even say it, but it's a conservative free market idea."[387] Business leaders may recognize the need for regulation to "level the playing field" and can adapt to and even profit from the regulations,[388] but politicians will try to associate regulations with job losses.

Commenting on the House committee, Democratic Rep. Henry Waxman observed, "The Republicans who run our committee deny the science. So there's not hope for legislation."[389] He mentioned the Obama policy of using the Clean Air Act to mandate reductions of greenhouse gas emissions from power plants, noting that the act has been vetted by the Supreme Court and requires no new legislation to implement.

Lamar Smith (R-TX), US House, chairman of the House Committee on Science, Space, and Technology, has also made statements about climate change "uncertainty." In an op-ed piece in the *Washington Post,* he stated, "Contrary to the claims of those who want to strictly regulate carbon dioxide emissions and increase the cost of energy for all Americans, there is a great amount of uncertainty associated with climate science."[390] Smith makes a number of misstatements about climate science. There is not a "great amount of uncertainty" about the basic findings of climate science; the IPCC has stated that these findings have a high level of confidence. The findings do not "limit our understanding of how anthropogenic emissions will affect future warming trends." They provide definite and rigorous understanding of future warming trends. Global temperatures have not held steady for the past 15 years; they have increased.

One of the problems with the reasoning of these committee chairmen is that they do not realize the inhibiting effect of their statements and their committees' actions (or lack of actions) on climate policy. Because the EPA is under attack and the Congress does not consider possible solutions such as a carbon tax, US climate policy has stagnated. What little is done by the EPA tends to be delayed and drawn out because of congressional opposition.

A leading denial politician, Sen. James Inhofe, also has invoked jobs and went further to deny that GHG are pollutants: "The best way to eliminate EPA's carbon regime is through an authorization bill. That's why I released the Energy Tax Prevention Act of 2011 with Rep. Fred Upton...If we want to make strides in improving public health, we won't do it by regulating carbon dioxide. It's not a pollutant—despite what [the] EPA says."[391]

Inhofe restates a major point of denial ideology, saying, "It's not a pollutant—despite what [the] EPA says." This argument follows directly from the denial argument that since greenhouse gases do not poison people directly, they are not pollutants. (See the section "National Politics" in this chapter for a detailed examination of this issue.) In a broader context, this argument means that regulation of greenhouse gases is optional, depending on your view of the threat of climate change. If doubts can be raised about the effects of greenhouse gases on the environment, regulation becomes an issue of contention because of its costs. "Merchants of doubt" have been effective in raising doubts about climate change.[392]

In 2012, 221 representatives sent a letter to the Office of Management and Budget in the White House opposing EPA greenhouse gas (GHG) regulations. They used the following arguments: "Forcing a transition to commercially unproven technologies could send thousands of US jobs overseas and raise electricity rates on families and seniors at a time when the nation can least afford it," the lawmakers wrote. "We respectfully ask that you stop EPA's GHG rule making because of the devastating impact it will have on jobs and the economy."[393]

The letter may accurately describe carbon capture and storage as "commercially unproven technology," but there are other technologies that are commercially proven. The issue of a "devastating impact on jobs and the economy" is a tendentious argument about the consequences of rule making—clean energies just as well could create jobs and improve the economy.

Some in the media echo these arguments. The *Wall Street Journal* expands the argument on jobs to indict the EPA for a multitude of economic sins. The *Wall Street Journal* claims that the EPA has "decided all of a sudden" that CO2 is a pollutant,[394] when it has actually been under consideration for a number of years, including during the administration of George W. Bush. The *WSJ* bases its analysis on the premise that EPA regulations are unnecessary and harmful. It uses a fundamental denial of climate science based on a belief that fossil fuels are not producing "pollutants" that cause global warming, a belief that reflects the interests of the fossil fuel industry.

Many politicians oppose the EPA; Republicans are not alone in fighting EPA regulations on greenhouse gas emissions. Sen. Joseph Manchin, a Democrat from West Virginia, contends that EPA regulations are not valid: "It's time that the EPA realizes it cannot regulate what has not been legislated," Manchin said in a statement. He conveniently ignores the Clean Air Act. "Our government was designed so that elected representatives are in charge of making important decisions, not bureaucrats. The simple fact is that the EPA is trying to seize more power than it should have, and must be stopped. I hope that Democrats and Republicans can come together to stop the EPA's jobs-destroying power grab."[395]

Manchin's statement reflects the denial argument that the Clean Air Act does not cover carbon emissions, despite the Supreme Court ruling in 2007 that it does. The legislative history of the Clean Air Act explicitly includes climate change, but politicians tend to disregard this fact when expressing denial ideology. They make denial statements that are premised on rejection of EPA findings that carbon emissions are pollution and constitute endangerment under the Clean Air Act.

Another argument used by opponents of EPA regulation is the presumed effect on energy prices. House Energy and Commerce Chairman Upton and Energy Subcommittee Chairman Ed Whitfield in 2011 sent fellow members of Congress a letter that reads in part:

> Whether through greenhouse gas regulation, permit delays, or permanent moratoriums, the White House

takes every opportunity to decrease access to safe and secure sources of oil and natural gas. Gasoline prices have climbed dramatically over the past three months. American consumers deal with this hardship every day, and as this poll indicates, the majority of respondents do not see the pain subsiding anytime soon.[396]

It is a common argument of politicians that gasoline prices reflect EPA regulation, when in fact they are based on many different factors, of which regulation is a minor part. Nevertheless, politicians seek to blame climate science for costly changes in lifestyles and justify their opposition with denial ideology. In this way, they appeal to public fears about a lower standard of living. Higher gasoline prices do have a negative effect on discretionary spending.

When the House Energy and Commerce Committee debated the Upton-Whitfield "Energy Tax Prevention" proposal, Republicans declined to vote for a Democratic amendment affirming the findings of climate science.[397] Republicans are constrained from supporting climate science and its implications for public health by their dependence on support from denial ideologues. The Tea Party caucus in the House has considerable sway, and this influence permeates the representatives' votes.

Some members of Congress disputed the "endangerment" finding the EPA used in writing regulations on climate change. These members filed a petition challenging the EPA greenhouse gas endangerment finding with the following text:

> The conclusions of organizing bodies, especially the IPCC, cannot be said to reflect scientific "consensus" in any meaningful sense of that word. Instead, they reflect a political movement that has commandeered science to the service of its agenda. This is "postnormal science": the long-dreaded arrival of deconstructionism to the natural sciences, according to which scientific quality is

determined not by its fidelity to truth, but by its fidelity to the political agenda.[398]

Denial advocates have developed the concept of "postnormal science" to distinguish climate science from other forms of science. They assert that climate scientists are driven by political motives and therefore do not apply principles of scientific validity used in "normal" science.

An additional argument used by denial ideologues is that the EPA is not the appropriate agency to regulate greenhouse gases. The argument asserts that because greenhouse gas emissions are so intertwined with energy and economic growth, Congress should regulate them: "The EPA is pursuing a dramatic shift in our nation's energy and environmental policy that would send shock waves through our economy. Setting the course of our energy policy is the job of Congress, not a single federal agency acting without authority."[399] This statement by Representative Whitfield conveniently overlooks the fact that Congress has had a major role in setting energy policy, including its previous actions on passing and amending the Clean Air Act. Whether the EPA has the authority has been a major point of contention, but with the imprimatur of the Supreme Court, it is dubious to argue flatly that it acts without authority.

Hearings on the "Energy Tax Prevention Act" bill involved a number of witnesses called by the Republican leadership. One of them, physicist Richard Muller of the Berkeley Earth Surface Temperature (BEST) project, surprised the committee when he did not support the denial presumptions of the leadership.[400] Apparently, the witness list backfired. Muller's lab had been supported by the Koch brothers, and that may have led politicians to expect that he would parrot denial ideology. As an honest scientist, he did not toe the denial line and instead reported that climate science is valid and that errors attributed to scientists are not compelling enough to reject the science. This conclusion may have been doubly troubling to the denial ideologues. He not only confirmed that climate science is sound, but also refuted the denial contention that scientists are fudging the data.

Muller's "heresy" has infuriated denial ideologues. Marc Morano, former staffer for Senator Inhofe and publisher of *Climate Depot*, reacted as follows: "*Climate Depot* since at least March of 2011 had been publicly warning that Muller's entire BEST project was a predetermined con set up to take down a straw man argument...He has allowed leaks, media distortions, allowed [Joe] Romm to publicly hijack [the] project, and Muller remains silent."[401] Apparently, when an apostate scientist confirms climate science, he is banished from the denial community. Denial activists accuse Muller, a respected physicist, of allowing leaks, media distortions, and the hijacking of his project.

Sometimes it is refreshing to inject a little humor into politics. One member introduced some facetious amendments to rename the "Energy Tax Prevention Act": the "Koch Brothers Appreciation Act," the "Middle Eastern Economic Development and Assistance Act," the "Head in the Sand Act" and the "Protecting Americans from Polar Bears Act."[402]

Republicans were not amused.

In addition to the "Energy Tax Prevention Act," Congress is considering the Natural Gas Act that would encourage the use of natural gas as an alternative to petroleum for fueling cars and trucks. T. Boone Pickens, a long-time energy entrepreneur who promotes wind energy for power generation and natural gas for vehicles, advocates the proposal. A provision of the act involves regulation of greenhouse gases. Section 403 of the bill reads:

> It is the sense of the Congress that the Environmental Protection Agency new fuel economy and greenhouse gas emission regulations for medium- and heavy-duty engines and vehicles should provide incentives to encourage and reward manufacturers who produce natural gas powered vehicles. Such regulations should take into account the petroleum reductions provided by such vehicles and also quantify all greenhouse gas emission reductions provided by natural gas powered engines and vehicles.

Because this act mentions greenhouse gas regulation, it has drawn the ire of conservative groups, who have persuaded some Republicans to withdraw support for the act. One of these conservative groups, the Club for Growth, accuses sponsors of supporting EPA efforts to regulate GHG emissions. The tendency of denial ideology to influence political decisions without regard to the merits of a proposal depends on how seriously a threat like this is taken. Even though the advocates of gas-fueled transportation and wind energy such as T. Boone Pickens have credibility as business leaders, and emphasize the rationale of energy independence, the opponents ignore this rationale and threaten any apostates with a "pro-Obama" label. The only thing that matters is that the bill mentions regulation, a taboo for many conservatives.

Another proposed law, titled TRAIN, for Transparency in Regulatory Analysis of Impacts on the Nation Act of 2011, was introduced by Rep. John Sullivan (R-OK). It would also limit EPA regulations of greenhouse gas emissions. The term "train wreck" is often used in denial ideology as a description for the presumed impact of EPA regulations on jobs and economic growth. Ideologues claim that the effect of regulations is so overwhelmingly negative that they would wreck the economy. While it is difficult to take such proposals seriously, there are implications for climate policy even if the proposal is not passed.

When government agencies attempt to provide climate information in a neutral manner, they are still subject to criticism by politicians. NOAA proposed to establish a Climate Service to consolidate reporting on climate conditions, but one member of Congress, Rep. Andy Harris (R-MD), took umbrage. He said, "On the topic of climate change, there's already evidence that the climate service could become a source of sensationalistic exaggeration instead of science."[403]

The Climate Service reports on historical and long-term weather patterns are used by industries such as shipping and agriculture to plan their activities. "Demand for such data is skyrocketing," NOAA Administrator Jane Lubchenco told Congress earlier this year. "Farmers are wondering when to plant. Urban planners want to know whether groundwater will stop flowing under subdivisions. Insurance companies need climate data to help them set rates."[404] It has a minor role in publicizing climate science and promotes no policy positions. Nevertheless, some politicians find it threatening to their denial beliefs. "Sensationalist exaggeration" is code for climate science projections of global warming problems, which politicians regard as objectionable. Even though such projections are no different in methodology than other models used in science, such as weather forecasting, they threaten the denial beliefs that climate will not change or will have no significant consequences.

A particularly inane example of congressional action is the introduction of a bill to defund IPCC (see chapter 1) and the UN Framework Convention on Climate Change. The bill was introduced by US Rep. Blaine Luetkemeyer (R-MO), who said, "The American people should not have to foot the bill for an international organization that is fraught with waste, engaged in dubious science, and is promoting an agenda that will destroy jobs and drive up the cost of energy in the United States."[405] Apparently, denial advocates such as Luetkemeyer do not want to know the facts about climate change because these facts would undermine their denial ideology.

The actions of House members illustrate a principal problem of climate policy: the polarization of climate politics. Only one house can vote down a proposal: The Climate Service bill was killed in the House by a vote of 184 to 240, so the Senate will not take it up. The reverse is also true: As of this writing, none of the other House bills passed the Senate or reached President Obama's desk for signature. Their main effect seems to have been to fulfill promises made to the Tea Party caucus and voters. This has the effect of putting climate policy into limbo, with no action by the federal government.

This polarization extends to electoral politics involving members of Congress. When Sen. Richard Lugar was defeated in a primary election in Indiana by Republican Richard Mourdock, Lugar lamented the fact that he was unable to even discuss climate change because its mention violated conservative orthodoxy. His victorious opponent, however, was able to label it "junk science."[406] Of course,

Mourdock, supported by the Tea Party, was able to use the denial canards "junk science" and "alarmism" to characterize climate science. That seems to be OK as long as there is no acknowledgment of the facts of climate change. Ironically, Mourdock's extremism cost the Republicans a Senate seat.

Kenneth Trenberth of the National Center for Atmospheric Research noted that "there is some concern that the political debate will hinder the scientific work still to be done." Trenberth pointed out that congressional budget cuts nixed the National Oceanic and Atmospheric Administration's plans to establish a national climate service, which would have drawn together disparate climate data and projects under one umbrella. "Setting up a climate service is actually a good management tool," Trenberth said. "The Congress has blindly struck out at anything that has 'climate' in it, and that's happening on Capitol Hill."[407] This means that scientific research has been caught up in political polarization, and the science can be damaged by denial ideology.

Climate politics is a volatile mixture of science, policy, and ideology. As noted in Bloomberg News, "Politicians have been known to dissemble about risk because voters generally don't like to hear bad news. The insurance industry makes its money telling it to you straight—how long you'll probably live, what price your home will fetch, whether to repair or trade in your car."[408] The reference to politicians is telling. One insurance executive told the Senate Committee on Environment and Public Works, "The industry is at great financial peril if it does not understand global and regional climate impacts, variability, and developing scientific assessment of a changing climate. We are committed to work with you to address the exposure of citizens and their property to extreme weather risk."[409] Despite this warning, some senators were not convinced. "Sen. David Vitter of Louisiana said the climate is always changing, and that solar flares, natural emissions of carbon dioxide, or cosmic rays may be the cause of current weather patterns."[410] He repeated the denial ideology claims that "the climate is always changing" and that only natural causes are involved. (See chapter 4 for more discussion of politicians.)

Business has a vested interest in assessing risk, and, as noted in the next chapter, many businesses are planning energy policies and disaster recovery on the basis of climate science. If politicians were to do the same, they would be instituting major climate policies now rather than delaying them or dissembling on the science. Business accepts the findings of climate science but finds the political system lacking in reality orientation, due largely to denial ideology.

Chapter 5.
Culture Conflict and Climate Politics

Conflict generated by denial ideology spills over into climate politics. The aftermath of recent elections is a Congress and a Republican Party with "Tea Party" principles and opposition to action on climate change. Some politicians may indeed be denial ideologues; others may only be fellow travelers. Their effect on the body politic will remain, even if they lose elections in the future. The consequence has been, and will continue to be, a polarization of the climate issue, posing jobs against emissions controls. While a false dichotomy, this framing of the issue will continue to poison politics for years, if not decades, to come.

A result of this polarization is culture conflict on an issue that should unify society. Science does not generate this conflict; only ideology can be so divisive. Prodded by denial ideology, politicians exploit culture conflict through misinformation for political gain. Nowhere is this more divisive than in the false beliefs on jobs and growth versus sustainability.

Jobs and Growth

Politicians rely on arguments about jobs and growth. These arguments are also used by many businesses, and they have been expanded by the US Chamber of Commerce to contend that EPA emissions rules delay or obstruct all energy projects.[411] The Chamber does acknowledge that there are "green" energy projects as well as conventional energy projects. Their argument assumes, however, that all energy jobs are equally beneficial, and that regulations are unnecessary burdens. This argument does not distinguish between the effects of coal-fired power plants versus solar or wind power on either the environment or the economy.

Some local business groups have attacked the US Chamber of Commerce for its position on climate change. When Aspen, Colorado, ski resorts had some of their worst snow seasons in history they tried to get the local chamber of commerce to separate from the national organization.[412] Here is a case where a local chamber of commerce has found that the livelihood of its members is threatened by global warming. As local groups see the effects of climate change firsthand, they are likely to let the national lobbying groups know that they have much more to lose from denial ideology than national groups realize.

Another voice in the denial approach to government regulation is the Heritage Foundation. It supports a proposal by Senator Barrasso (R-WY), which cites a number of acts that could hinder "affordable energy and jobs."[413] Barrasso would use congressional action to preempt EPA regulation of a number of environmental problems. The wholesale preemption of regulation is an approach that appeals to some business interests. The Heritage Foundation introduces the argument of "regulatory certainty," as if government regulations somehow mean uncertainty. This is not the view of many businesses that have operated profitably under regulations in the past.[414]

Business Views on Climate

Government regulation of energy and emissions is an issue for businesses. Not all businesses agree that regulation is problematic; in fact, many look to regulation to provide the certainty needed for long-term investments.[415] Since they are realistic about the future, many businesses find denial ideology distasteful. "We cannot risk our kids' futures on the false hope that the vast majority of scientists are wrong," according to several major companies that issued a joint call for the United States to enact legislation to battle climate change, saying that the issue was critical to their businesses.[416] Businesses not only talk the talk, they walk the walk.[417] There are many examples of businesses that are addressing climate change.

Walmart, one of the largest businesses in the world, would rank ninth in the global economy if it were a nation. Until 2005, Walmart had a reputation for being antienvironmental, and it still has the image of a disreputable business among some environmentalists. When CEO Lee Scott embraced sustainability concepts and practices in 2005, however, Walmart become an environmental advocate and took up the cause of combating climate change.[418] The "Sustainable Value Networks" program at Walmart emphasizes energy efficiency and renewable energies. Some stores have solar panels and skylights; the efficiency of the truck fleet and refrigeration displays at many stores has increased; and Walmart has promoted the sale of compact fluorescent bulbs in place of incandescents. Suppliers have been evaluated for sustainable business practices, and Walmart has introduced organic food and clothing.[419] All of these changes have been made in the name of profit and lower prices, giving the lie to those who say that sustainability increases costs.

Unfortunately, Walmart's actions may be overwhelmed by its growth. While reductions in per-store emissions and improvements in the supply chain are laudable, increases in the number of stores and in total sales will overcome the decrease in emissions by individual stores or suppliers.[420] This is one of the ironies of growth, the Jevons paradox: as efficiencies reduce use of energy and resources for each unit, the total use of energy and resources increases.

Business's concern with denial of climate change is not confined to one company or sector. It is spreading across the business world as more and more business leaders recognize the risks. As former Energy Secretary Stephen Chu said to his employees in his 2013 departure letter, "In the last two years, the private sector, including Warren Buffett, Bank of America, Wells Fargo, and Google, has announced major investments in clean energy. Originally skeptical lenders and investors now see that renewable energy will be profitable." These investors are voting where it counts the most—with their wallets. As one CEO recently commented, "Solar is now bankable. When solar was perceived as more risky it required a premium."[421] Insurance companies and others have also recognized the need to manage the risks of climate change.[422]

Insurance is one of the most sensitive barometers of climate risk; as the risks increase, so will premiums.

Another business that is highly sensitive to increased fossil fuel emissions is the shellfish industry. Oystermen and crab fisheries know firsthand the effects of acidification of the oceans. They are like the canaries in the coal mine among businesses—they feel the first effects and their businesses are adversely affected. Shells of juvenile clams, oysters, and crabs do not grow well in acidified water, and the juveniles die soon after hatching. One oysterman said, "I don't care if you think it's the fault of humans or not, that's up to you. But the rest of us need to get it together because we're not out of the woods yet on this thing."[423] Oystermen and crab fishers in the Pacific Northwest cannot afford denial ideology; it ruins their business.

Many businesses recognize that reducing greenhouse gas emissions is not only good for the environment; it is also good for profits. Reduction of energy costs often goes directly to the bottom line. IBM, for example, saved $791 million from reduced energy costs during the 12 years from 1990 to 2002, and Dupont used 9% less energy during the same period.[424]

Although business leaders recognize the benefits of reducing emissions, the business press has a political agenda and often sides with denial politicians. One tendentious argument used by the business press is that the responsibility of any one source for worldwide emissions is impossible to assess. The *Wall Street Journal*, for example, claims:

> It is impossible to determine whether emissions by any
> particular power plant—or US electricity production as
> a whole—have affected warming trends and, if so, how.
> Nor can we surmise what party is responsible in whole
> or in part for the particular plaintiffs' alleged injuries.[425]

This claim, in an editorial written about a 2011 Supreme Court case involving a "nuisance" claim, contends that it is impossible to determine emissions from any particular power plant or even the electricity sector as a whole, an argument that is false on its face.[426] Carbon emissions can be measured for individual plants and the sector, which is in fact the basis of EPA regulations.[427] The EPA conveniently provides an online list and map of all of the individual plants in the United States.[428] The effect of specific levels of CO_2 emissions on climate change has also been documented.[429] In other words, it is possible to assess "whether emissions by any particular power plant—or US electricity production as a whole—has affected warming trends and, if so, how." That is precisely what the EPA and the Energy Department are doing. When the *Wall Street Journal* ignores this information, it is either failing to check facts or deliberately using denial ideology.

Perhaps the most extreme and extensive argument about regulations, jobs, and growth is that of Mario Loyola, a former counsel to the US Senate Republican Policy Committee and aide to Sen. James Inhofe.[430] He collects a number of arguments used in denial ideology. He belittles the effects of the regulations while emphasizing their costs. He lays out a number of problems that are attributed to EPA regulations, including reduction of investment, decrease in GDP, increases in transportation costs, leading to higher food prices, and shutdown of restaurants and apartment buildings. He treats CO_2 as a nonpollutant, which, because people exhale CO_2, would limit buildings to 250 occupants—a rather creative interpretation of the regulations.

One reason that denial ideologues argue that CO_2 is not a pollutant is attempted persuasion of those who regard pollutants as "abnormal" gases not usually found in the atmosphere. CO_2, after all, has been around for billions of years. CO_2 is sometimes considered a beneficial gas, as it promotes plant growth, but only in natural concentrations well below 1% of the atmosphere. In higher concentrations, of course, CO_2 can be poisonous, as was the case when 1,700 residents near Lake Nyos in Cameroon suffocated from a high concentration in the air. As CO_2 concentrations climb, they will have much more severe effects when climate change brings droughts, floods, and severe weather. Since these disasters result from a gradual increase in the concentrations, however, they are not seen to be as dangerous as the other kinds of pollution. Eventually, however, they will be more dangerous; plants will stop growing in droughts and high temperatures, and many other consequences will endanger life.

An unanticipated consequence of enhanced plant growth is increased health costs from asthma and allergy. These costs are associated with the higher pollen counts caused by the rise in CO_2 emissions. Pollen counts doubled during the last century and are expected to double again this century.[431] Temperature increases have also lengthened the growing season in northern areas such as Minnesota and Chicago, where higher levels of allergenic plants, such as ragweed, are occurring.[432] Carbon dioxide is not the unmitigated blessing that some denial ideologues claim.

Countering the Denial Arguments

Most of the arguments used by politicians and the business press to deny climate change can be countered with data. The argument on jobs is the most common, because an argument can be made that a sound climate policy creates jobs, rather than destroying them. Take the example of California: implementation of its cap-and-trade system can reduce CO_2 emissions by 80%, increase state income by $76 billion, and create up to 403,000 new jobs.[433] Of course, there will be displacement of workers in the fossil fuel sector if regulations result in cutbacks in energy produced from fossil fuels. Compared to fossil fuel industry jobs, however, alternative energy jobs are more numerous per unit of energy produced. Further, the decline in fossil fuel industry jobs already is occurring for other reasons.[434]

Another argument used by denial ideologues is that greenhouse gas emissions are not unhealthy. The EPA used an "endangerment" finding to argue that greenhouse gas emissions are pollutants because of their ultimate effect on health. The argument that EPA regulations are unnecessary because greenhouse emissions do not create a public health danger is found in denial statements such as the NIPCC (described in chapter 1).[435] Scientists, however, attribute adverse health effects to lethal heat waves, spreading insect-borne disease, and decline of ecosystem services.[436] The World Health Organization has confirmed this view of the effect of climate on public health, citing threats to clean air, safe drinking water, sufficient food, and secure shelter.[437] Probably the most unhealthful thing about climate change is the effect it has on food production. Famines and malnutrition are particularly deadly.[438]

Of course, specific weather events and even trends have multiple causes, but it is clear that climate change is occurring and food security is becoming less assured. In addition, diseases associated with climate change are increasing. These statements are supported by extensive research. Diseases such as asthma, dengue fever, Lyme disease, and malaria all are exacerbated by climate change. Plant pathogens, including insects, fungus, and heat, reduce crop yields, leading to malnutrition and starvation.[439] In other words, CO_2 emissions do not contribute to plant growth in the way that some denial ideologues claim; their net effect is to make agriculture "more vulnerable" and threaten food security. "Climate change endangers crop and livestock yields and the health of fisheries and forests at the very same time that surging populations worldwide are placing new demands on food production."[440]

Microsoft, the company Bill Gates founded, enabled the establishment of the Gates Foundation. Its work is concerned with global health issues. A company spokesman said: *"Microsoft believes climate change is a serious issue that demands immediate, worldwide attention, and we are acting accordingly."* This principle led Microsoft to adopt "a broad policy statement on climate change that expresses support for government action to create market-based mechanisms to address climate change."[441] Microsoft made this statement in response to accusations that the company contributed to the Heartland Institute, a denial organization (see chapter 2). Microsoft in fact contributes free software to most nonprofit organizations that request it, and Heartland qualified by virtue of some of its other programs as well as climate denial. But Microsoft has distanced itself from Heartland in the wake of the Heartland billboard scandal: Heartland "does not speak for Microsoft on climate change. In fact, the Heartland Institute's position on climate change is diametrically opposed to Microsoft's position. And we completely disagree with the group's inflammatory and distasteful advertising campaign."[442]

ExxonMobil has had a striking evolution of views on climate change. In the 1990s, then CEO Lee Raymond reacted rather strongly to the IPCC Second Assessment Report: "Lee Raymond publicly rejected even the qualified formulations of the 1995 assessment...[with] the argument that evidence about man-made climate change was an illusion and that a binding agreement to reduce greenhouse gas emissions was therefore unnecessary."[443] During Raymond's leadership, ExxonMobil supported a number of denial organizations and fought climate policies in the United States. He used the denial argument of development versus mitigation to urge developing countries to reject mitigation policies.[444] ExxonMobil joined with other fossil fuel companies and auto companies to form the Global Climate Coalition, with the purpose of defeating any effective emissions controls. It supported the Heartland Institute's programs of denial.

Rex Tillerson replaced Lee Raymond in 2006, and ExxonMobil's approach to climate change began to change. At first it was rather gradual and involved mainly a change in personnel. Tillerson decided to change the Washington office staff and dismissed some of the deniers. On January 9, 2009, Tillerson made a speech in Washington that changed the ExxonMobil position dramatically. "For the first time in ExxonMobil's century-long history, its chairman went on to advocate that the government impose higher taxes on oil and gas use, to reduce the risks posed by climate change."[445] In the speech, Tillerson said: "There is another policy option that should be considered, and that is a carbon tax. As a businessman, it is hard to speak favorably about any new tax. But a carbon tax strikes me as a more direct, a more transparent, and a more effective approach.[446]

ExxonMobil has come a long way since Lee Raymond's denial position, and the company now acknowledges the need for a climate policy. Tillerson did more than "talk the talk"; he "walked the walk" by reducing ExxonMobil's carbon footprint. ExxonMobil has drawn the ire of a number of environmentalists because of some of its past support for denial movements. After the change of leadership in 2006, however, ExxonMobil also changed its approach to climate change. "ExxonMobil supports adopting strategies for reducing emissions that are stable, predictable, long term, simple, and transparent—and that encourage the greatest reduction in emissions at the least possible cost to society."[447] ExxonMobil does qualify its support by calling for a market-based approach to climate change, but its support for global participation and flexibility is a sound policy position.

Regardless of the future effect of ExxonMobil's change of heart, its past support of denial ideology will have a lasting effect on policy. It continues to support organizations such as ALEC (American Legislative Exchange Council; see chapter 4 for more details). Greenpeace has reported that ExxonMobil continues to fund at least twelve denial groups.[448] As in the case of so many organizations involved in denial of climate change, ExxonMobil has invested much time and many resources in fending off the facts, only to find that its position is untenable. "Exxon has scaled back its annual anti-climate-science funding by 78%, or $2.7 million, since 2006."[449] When it comes to the realization that climate science is valid and has serious consequences, ExxonMobil changes its risk management strategies and switches positions. Its past positions, however, still reverberate through think tanks and "AstroTurf" organizations it previously funded.

ExxonMobil still has reservations about the science. By assessing climate models as "pretty limited," Tillerson expresses one of the tenets of denial ideology.[450] Of course, no scientist would claim that models are "unlimited," but Tillerson's reservation implies that one can dismiss the more drastic projections and treat the consequences as "manageable." With regard to climate modeling research at the Massachusetts Institute of Technology (MIT), Tillerson said: "We've been working with a very good team at MIT now for more than 20 years on this area of modeling the climate…The competencies of the models are not particularly good." MIT researcher Ronald Prinn disputed his assessment: "The models are certainly good enough to clearly show the benefits of mitigation policies compared to no policy in lowering risks."[451]

Tillerson repeats one of the canards of denial ideology: models do not perfectly predict temperature increases or other effects of climate change, and policies should not be based on such "imperfect" models. Of course "all models are wrong," but "some are useful...the central message [is] the direction and approximate magnitude of change."[452] If we wait until all of the models are perfectly "right" and reality bears them out, it will be too late. Tillerson also reflects the denial ideology in his treatment of climate change as a low priority. He echoes the Lomborg analysis that makes alleviation of poverty a higher priority. Tillerson repeats the false dichotomy of emissions limits vs. poverty alleviation, a dichotomy that has been refuted by a number of studies.[453]

Other oil company executives have come to realize that the future of their own businesses depends on understanding the risks of climate change. John Hofmeister, former president of the Shell Oil Company in the United States, noted that the industry has plenty of reserves: "The resources are there. The question is: Do we want to continue to use these fossil fuels at current—or increasing—rates until they are eventually exhausted? The answer, unequivocally, is no. The economic, social, and environmental costs of such an approach are becoming ever clearer and ever higher."[454] Even though oil executives must be concerned about stranded assets—oil identified in reserves that cannot be extracted—the risks of climate change are too great to ignore.

Businesses rise and fall on the strength of their risk management. Agriculture is an area of business where risk management is paramount. One way that climate change affects agriculture is to make prices more volatile, impacting the food market.[455] Of course, biofuel production has been touted as a route to energy independence, but it does not reduce carbon emissions by much, if at all. Biofuel production presently requires large energy inputs from fossil fuels, and the net return on energy invested is about zero. The severe hot conditions of recent droughts reduce agricultural production regardless of the increase in production that some denial ideologues claim CO_2 enhances.[456] "Even one or two degrees of global warming is likely to substantially increase heat waves that lead to low-yield years and more price volatility," said

Noah Diffenbaugh of Stanford University in California.[457] Agriculture is the segment of business most affected by climate change. The American Farm Bureau Federation, a lobbying organization that purportedly represents farmers, has opposed climate legislation. National Farm Bureau spokesman Mace Thornton said, "We're not convinced that the climate change we're seeing is anthropogenic in origin. We don't think the science is there to show that in a convincing way."[458] The Farm Bureau seems to think that the only effect of climate legislation is to impose immediate costs on farmers and ranchers.[459] Apparently they are not concerned that inaction could impose more costs on agriculture in the long run.

Severe droughts in 2012 reduced the corn and wheat crops in the Midwest, leading to higher food prices and culling of cattle herds. When asked about the causes of the drought, Secretary of Agriculture Tom Vilsack hesitated to attribute it to climate change.[460] Apparently Vilsack is hesitant because denial ideology espoused by other politicians impedes him from offering an "opinion" on the drought. While the IPCC and NOAA have identified climate change as a contributing factor in droughts, Vilsack did not want to go there at his press conference. Previously, Vilsack had acknowledged the possibility of climate change drought effects, but he seemed to be unwilling to cross organizations like the Farm Bureau on the issue.

Farmers are not so sure that the Farm Bureau's position is the right one for the industry to take, however. When surveyed by the Iowa Extension Service, farmers indicated that they were worried about climate change and needed to prepare for its effects, such as heavy precipitation.[461] Farmers in the survey seem uncertain about impacts of climate change, but they are aware that there may be flooding, droughts, and other changes in weather patterns. This is a prudent position for farmers to take, even if they do not understand all of the ramifications of climate change.

Much of the attention of politicians opposing controls on greenhouse emissions focuses on the scope of the Clean Air Act. Scientists have defended the application of the Clean Air Act to climate policy and accused Republicans of trying to weaken it. Lexi Shultz, legislative director of the Climate and Energy Program at the Union of Concerned Scientists (UCS), labeled the House Republicans' "Energy Tax Prevention Act" an "Orwellian" proposal because it uses the term "tax" when no taxes are proposed.[462]

Scientists advocate using the Clean Air Act for regulation of greenhouse gas emissions in addition to the other gases regulated by the act, such as ozone, sulfur dioxide, nitrous oxides, and particulates. For some contrarians, it is a stretch because greenhouse gases such as CO_2 and methane are "natural" products of combustion or decay and, as such, are not considered poisons. CO_2 is measured in parts per million and methane in parts per billion in normal atmosphere; these small concentrations lead lay observers to conclude that they are not dangerous. As scientists have indicated, however, these small amounts can have cumulative effects.[463] Their effects are not immediate; but the long-term effects include dangers such as floods, droughts, and extreme weather events.

Many scientists anticipate public health threats from floods, droughts, and decreased food production, but it is difficult to predict when and where any of these specific threats will occur. Linking any of them directly to climate change is dicey at best and opens climate science to attacks from denial ideologues. The scientific difficulties of establishing a link between climate change and health were highlighted by the Office of the Inspector General (OIG) of the EPA, which said that the EPA's endangerment finding "thus required a more rigorous EPA peer review than occurred."[464]

Of course, denial advocates immediately seized on this report to claim that the EPA does not have a basis for its endangerment finding. Senator Inhofe released a statement:

> This report confirms that the endangerment finding, the very foundation of President Obama's job-destroying regulatory agenda, was rushed, biased, and flawed. It calls the scientific integrity of [the] EPA's decision-making

process into question and undermines the credibility of the endangerment finding. The endangerment finding is no small matter: global warming regulations imposed by the Obama EPA under the Clean Air Act will cost American consumers $300 [billion] to $400 billion a year, significantly raise energy prices, and destroy hundreds of thousands of jobs. This is not to mention the "absurd result" that EPA will need to hire 230,000 additional employees and spend an additional $21 billion to implement its greenhouse gas regime.[465]

Inhofe repeats the denial arguments about costs of GHG regulations, flaws in the science, and destruction of jobs. These heavy accusations are all hung precariously on a rather small hook of criticism of procedures used by the EPA.

When a court of appeals upheld the EPA jurisdiction based on the Clean Air Act endangerment provision, Senator Inhofe responded: "[The] EPA's massive and complicated regulatory barrage will continue to punish job creators and further undermine our economy."[466] Inhofe's response echoes that of conservative business leaders: "The EPA's decision to move forward with these regulations is one of the most costly, complex, and burdensome regulations facing manufacturers," said Jay Timmons, president of the National Association of Manufacturers. "These regulations will harm their ability to hire, invest, and grow."[467] To assume that the regulations will automatically add burdens to businesses is an egregious vulgarization of the regulatory process and distorts the views of most businesses.[468]

EPA has used valid sources of scientific data to justify its endangerment finding.[469] Further, there are indications that opponents seize on any straw to exaggerate the effects of regulations. Inhofe's claim that the EPA "will need to hire 230,000 additional employees and spend an additional $21 billion to implement its greenhouse gas regime" is based on a false report.[470] Once again, we see the denialsphere echoing misinformation from a canard created out of whole cloth. Nevertheless, the reports went "viral" and appeared on a number of news outlets, including Fox News.[471] These false reports beg the questions: Will the corrections or retractions catch up with the original reports? What damage will they cause before corrections are made?

With regard to the "Energy Tax Prevention Act," the Obama White House also indicated its opposition to the Republican proposal. Its counterarguments are based on a number of contentions, including health and energy efficiency, and the White House calls for fuel efficiency standards and threatens to veto the bill.[472]

All of this culture conflict tends to exacerbate the political conflict over climate change. What are the effects of these counterarguments? Let us examine three areas of political conflict.

1. *Public Opinion:* It is not clear that there is a direct effect on public opinion, but over the years substantial majorities (60%–80%) have supported some aspects of climate policy. It is not always clear if they support specific policies, however. One can question whether Congress reflects the "will of the people" in its efforts to strip the EPA of the power to regulate greenhouse gases. According to a public opinion poll, people trust the EPA more than Congress.[473] Voters realize that climate policy is better managed by experts than by members of Congress, who are subject to pressures from denial advocates.

2. *Regulation:* Another arena of debate is in the business sector. As we have seen, many businesses accept and even embrace regulation when they realize that it provides certainty.[474] Specific sectors, however, may see problems with specific regulations. The electric utilities, for example, seem to be ambivalent about EPA regulation. When a case involving lawsuits by a number of states came before the Supreme Court, they argued that the EPA should have responsibility; in Congress, they argue the opposite.[475]

3. *Free Markets:* According to some economists, the free market solves environmental problems through pricing mechanisms. Ironically, this may actually occur after climate change raises energy prices drastically and undermines the growth of energy-dependent economies.[476] This is not what the advocates of free markets anticipate,

but it may be the outcome of their ideological judgments. By delaying action on climate change, they are making eventual responses much more difficult and costly, burdening the market with much higher costs of adaptation.

One of the problems with the market system is that the prices are not accurate signals of costs. As an apt analogy, author Lester Brown compares the use of "free" market pricing to Enron Corporation, which became bankrupt because of faulty accounting.[477] The irony of "free" markets is that they treat as "free" the social and environmental costs of resources such as oil and gas. In economics terminology, this is "externalizing" by pricing resources in a way that cleaves off their true costs. Some economists would argue that pollution, including greenhouse gases, constitutes a market failure. If fossil fuels were priced at their real cost, including health costs and costs of adaptation to climate change, they would be priced at multiples of their current prices. Such pricing would open up the market for renewable energies, but, as critics warn, it would also exacerbate problems of poverty and development. Denial ideology emphasizes prices because of their presumed effects on economic growth and standards of living. If they fully reflect energy costs, prices may have some negative effects on growth and may cause economic dislocations. This does not mean that long-term effects will be negative, however. With proper price signals, markets may adjust early enough to avoid some of the deleterious effects of climate change.

With regard to international climate policy, there are a number of counterarguments to the denial position. Most denial ideologues argue that, in addition to being unnecessary, climate policy disadvantages American companies and workers. Denial movement leaders have criticized the Kyoto Protocol as a form of "world government," and environmentalists have criticized it as too weak. While it is true that the Kyoto Protocol goals are not ambitious enough to meet the criteria of some scientists,[478] they are the first step in a series of efforts that will be needed. Along with the target of 5% reduction in GHG emissions, the Kyoto Protocol has had some other beneficial effects.[479] It has spurred energy efficiency in Europe and Asia and made companies there more competitive. When US companies use twice as much energy per unit of GDP as European and Asian competitors, they are losing the competitive race, not because of lack of adherence to the Kyoto Protocol but because the indirect effects of the protocol are giving the Europeans and Asians competitive advantages. They have vastly improved energy efficiency. This is what Lovins and Cohen mean by saying that climate change is a challenge of capitalism.[480]

While Republicans embrace much of the denial ideology, climate science is not a partisan issue. Among the Republicans who have, in the past, argued in favor of cap-and-trade policies for climate change are John McCain and Newt Gingrich. Many Republicans do have problems with the ideological positions of denial movements.[481] In the past, conservation and conservative political views were complementary. Conservative presidents such as Theodore Roosevelt (parks and forests), Richard Nixon (Clean Air Act, Clean Water Act, EPA), Ronald Reagan (ozone protocol), and George H. W. Bush (climate change convention) supported conservation causes. While Republicans have conservative heroes who were conservationists, today the party seems to have adopted a nonconservationist Tea Party conservatism. This brand of conservatism makes a radical separation between preservation of human society and institutions, on one hand, and preservation of natural systems on the other, not understanding that the former depend on the latter. Conservatism has thus become more aligned with denial ideology in the United States. In the rest of the world, conservatism does not have this orientation.[482] Unfortunately, in the United States, conservatism has a much more rigid approach to issues based on ideology.

In one sense, "conservative" is a label that should be applied to climate scientists, not politicians. Climate scientists tend to hedge their predictions and, for example, project sea-level rise at a more modest level than has actually occurred. Denial ideology may damage the application of climate science by making policies less positive than warranted by the data. The label "radical" should be applied to politicians who deny climate change; they are gambling with our future on a very tendentious basis of denial ideology.

Liberals, on the other hand, sometimes favor rapid economic development to alleviate poverty, and they may overlook the environmental costs of development. Most liberals, however, acknowledge that economic development has to take account of the preservation of natural systems. At present, this ideology tends to be defensive. The reduction of public support for climate policies—due to both apathy and disbelief in climate science—has had its effect at the ballot box, where conservative members of the House have gained strength and pushed leaders such as Upton and Speaker John Boehner toward denial. After President Obama proposed regulations for power plants and energy efficiency, Boehner said, "I think this is absolutely crazy. Why would you want to increase the cost of energy and kill more American jobs at a time when [the] American people are asking, 'Where are the jobs?' "[483] Boehner's leadership of what President Obama called the "flat earth society" is evidence of denial in Congress: Republicans have continued to ignore science in their pursuit of "jobs, jobs, and jobs."

In a more profound sense, the *conservation* movement has the real conservative ideology. It is, after all, the aim of the movement to conserve the world as it is, albeit with its main focus on the natural world rather than the political or economic world. Denial ideology is really a radical ideology, with its unstated aim of transforming the natural world drastically in the pursuit of economic growth. The unintended consequence of this transformation will be destruction of the natural base of growth and a decline in human prosperity.

Denial Redux

Despite all evidence to the contrary, denial ideology hangs on and continues to influence decision making. Climate science, professional economists, business leaders, and environmentalists have debunked all of the arguments, but ideologues hold on to their denial tenaciously. Chapter 3 described some of the reasons, but for this final section we need to deal with some of the issues of culture conflict and climate politics that continue to defy rational explanation.

A peculiar justification of denial is the concept that economic growth enables adaptation to climate change if and when it occurs. This view is developed by Patrick Michaels, one of the leading lights of the denial movement. Here is his take on hurricane intensity: "How silly it seems to take resources away in futile attempts to stop global 'warming.' Then those same resources can be directed toward adaptation, including infrastructure and hurricane-proof housing."[484]

A view like this is based on an "either-or" argument: either we put resources into mitigation ("stop global 'warming' ") or into adaptation. The working assumption is that growth will be possible only with unhindered free market capitalism, and mitigation by restricting GHG emissions will undermine this growth.

One result of this ethical conundrum is polarization of political culture as the two sides propound opposing ethical judgments. While the conservation ethic emphasizes the preservation of natural systems and resources as the basis of human life, the denial ethic promotes the use of energy to enable growth leading to the reduction of poverty and disease. In reality, these are not polar opposites, but in political culture they are seen as irreconcilable differences. Often the polarization is framed in terms of jobs, with the denial adherents claiming that regulation of greenhouse gases would "kill" jobs and the conservation adherents claiming that regulation would create new energy jobs. Both sides view the issue through the ideological lens of denial or conservation. As a result, they tend to move toward more fixed positions in the face of changing reality.

An effect of polarization is that ideology trumps facts. "Partisan disagreements are now so wide, and the ideological outlooks of activists and elected officials so antithetical, that there is no agreement on the facts, on what is true and what is false."[485] Climate scientists do their best to establish facts about global warming, but denial ideology makes it unlikely that all politicians will accept these facts. To quote Daniel Moynihan, they are "entitled to their own opinions, but not their own facts."

Severe storms in the United States in 2011 and 2012 killed hundreds of people and left wide swaths of destruction. While no climate scientist would link any specific event to climate change, some looked at global warming as a possible explanation. This elicited an absolutist response from the denial proponents.[486] The denial ideology leads *Human Events* to label climate science as "junk science" and accuse scientists of having a "twisted agenda." The strong language indicates ideological polarization and makes the debate rather brittle. It is difficult for opponents to agree on anything when the rhetoric is so divisive.

Ideological instability drives social change in response to climate change. As the ideologies are tested by real-world events and trends, they may be modified or discarded, and the movements that espouse them will wax or wane accordingly. The denial movements are likely to feel the pressure to change most, as they espouse an ideology based on denying reality.

Our concern about loss—losing our future because of climate catastrophes, or losing our standard of living—is the main issue of climate change policy. In future years, denial may lose credibility as consequences of climate change become more severe, but this will not stop the denial tendencies. As denial ideology becomes less relevant and less valid, the movement becomes more desperate; the effects of denial ideology on societies will still shape our future. That future may indeed be grim if the politics of denial continue to prevent needed changes.

Chapter 6.
Climate Denial and Social Change:
A Personal View

Many writers have suggestions for combatting climate change. When you read many of the books in the bibliography (below), you find a series of suggestions for addressing the problems of energy use and adaptation. I am not going to repeat these policy prescriptions because this book is more about the denial ideologies that relate to climate change and the movements that hold these ideologies. I will concentrate in this last chapter on tactics to combat denial. My purpose here is to identify the issues raised by denial ideology in a way that enables refutation of denial.

What to Do

You can change the light bulbs in your home. You can buy a hybrid or electric car, or take public transit. You can become a vegetarian and reduce the amount of energy needed to produce your food. All of these will make a difference in carbon emissions if you are joined by billions of people around the world. But what if there are no strong incentives for everyone to do the same? All of your efforts will have little effect on the climate. It is only when entire societies and the international community adopt emission reduction incentives that the problems will be solved. Encouraging this change requires rolling back the forces of denial.

Massive incentives are needed for emissions reductions sufficient enough to stabilize the climate. For example, if it were national or international policy that consumers pay full price for energy, and that the difference between the true price and retail costs be refunded to those who use less energy, there would be incentives for everyone to reduce energy consumption. Similarly, if fossil fuel prices reflected their true costs, consumers would pay higher prices for gasoline or electricity generated from coal, and rapid development of renewable energies could be subsidized. A carbon tax could be instituted to price goods and services appropriately.[487] None of this is feasible with the current political systems in place in most countries. I think that there are some actions that can be taken to address the political problems described here, however.

The first and most obvious thing that can address the problems of climate change ideology is to fully inform yourself about the issues. While it is tempting to ignore a problem that seems so remote, it is not an option if you want your children and grandchildren to have a future. It is not an issue on which you can remain neutral, and if you want to counter denial, you should know what to say. The books and articles listed in the reference list below are drawn from all points along the spectrum, from full denial to apologies for the denial movements to complete rejection of denial ideology. Many of the books and some of the articles also list the scientific findings that are attacked or supported by one or more of the movements. The most succinct review of climate science is the book by Kerry Emanuel, *What We Know About Climate Change.* Most of the scientific discussion is not highly technical and can be understood by an educated layperson. It is important, however, to understand that climate science is being undermined by denial ideology and to know which findings are attacked. Therefore, you should also read the denial books, particularly those by Michaels and Balling, Spencer, and Sussman.

A second approach is to cast a critical eye on the popular press description of issues. Articles in the press range from full denial to full support of climate science, but some will attempt to balance the issues by citing both sides. Use of the "balanced" approach, appropriate for many issues, is inappropriate for this issue. Even more egregious is the unbalanced approach, such as that promoted by "fair and balanced" Fox News.[488] You may have to respond to Fox viewers who are completely convinced of the validity of denial ideology. Virtually none of the denial ideology has any scientific credibility. It is no accident that denial ideologues attack the scientists rather than the science. They cannot disprove the science, so they try to denigrate the scientists. Some scientists have even received death threats. You should counter any attacks on scientists by asking, what have they said that makes them objects of attack? Any reports of science should be viewed skeptically; valid science can withstand critical review, but the denial ideology does not allow for a valid criticism of the science. Reviewing mass media reports critically does not imply that they are invalid or willing tools of denial ideology. They should be called to task, however, if the presentation implies that there is scientific validity on both sides.

A third approach to the issue is to look for signs of changes in society and one's personal circumstances. Energy prices are an obvious sign of changes. It is no accident that in recent years, prices of gasoline and other fossil fuels have escalated. While these prices have both a "signal" and "noise"—a steady increase in costs, versus the volatility of periodic ups and downs—the clear trend is upward. This will mean adjustments in personal consumption as well as a different view of lifestyles. It does not necessarily mean a lower standard of living, but understanding of what is important may change. Remember that denial is not always explicit or conscious. If someone is denying that there will be change, it is not necessarily because he or she is adhering to denial ideology. He or she may be unaware of the role of unconscious motives, especially fear of change. You can ask questions about energy use and extreme weather events, questions that may arouse curiosity about climate.

A fourth factor to watch is discontinuity in economic and social changes. Upfront costs of solar panels, wind energy, superinsulated houses, and electric cars are different calculations than the normal patterns of energy and durables markets. Most people are accustomed to paying mass-market prices for autos, appliances, and houses, and then paying continuously higher costs for fuel, electricity, and heating. The newer technologies require a different mind-set. Financing for major purchases and retrofitting of buildings will have to take into account future escalating energy costs of fossil fuels versus alternative sources of energy. This will require new types of finance, such as leases or loans paid off from energy savings. One author has suggested, half seriously, that all autos, appliances, and houses be sold with a prepaid energy card. Thus, for example, a 75-watt incandescent light bulb would come with a $60 prepaid electricity card. A new SUV would come with a $22,000 gasoline card. A new home would come with a $240,000 energy card. Of course, these prices would not be very popular, but they would in fact alert people to the real costs of energy. They might choose a Prius ($6,800 gasoline card) rather than a Chevy Suburban ($22,000 card).[489] Denying these costs in current culture is convenient and unwitting, but making them explicit could change attitudes. You can ask salesmen about energy costs when making a purchase.

Policy Options

On the national and international level, new approaches are needed as well. "Cap-and-trade" has been vilified by denial ideologues. Republicans, including President George H. W. Bush, first proposed it for reduction of sulfur dioxide emissions. While it is still considered a highly successful application of market economics to environmental policy, it has become politically toxic. Other approaches, including regulation and carbon taxes, are being tried at the national level in some countries. Some mix of approaches may be needed to achieve political and economic feasibility. The Kyoto Protocol under the UN Framework Convention on Climate Change is not considered highly effective. "Whether the developed nations that are signatories to the Kyoto accords hit their targets by buying real emissions reductions or 'hot air,' there is little evidence to date to show that the Kyoto limits-based approach alone will succeed in actually reducing real emissions significantly in the developed world."[490] New types of agreements, perhaps involving less than the full membership of UNFCCC, may be needed.[491] How these agreements are framed and what changes they lead to are major uncertainties in the future of social reactions to climate change. Regardless of how the UNFCCC negotiations proceed, they will need to change direction to achieve success.

As individuals, we do not have much influence over corporate, national, or international policies in the short run. We can vote for candidates who might promote certain policies, but they in turn are subject to pressures and influences that constrain their power to change society. Most politicians react to changes rather than direct them proactively, and it is this reactive stance that will determine the future course of social change. As the climate changes, politicians and diplomats will find themselves under increasing pressure to make the social and economic changes necessary to adapt to the new environment. If we understand how these dynamics work, we can better adapt our personal mind-set and behavior to the larger forces at work in the social and natural environment. Our most important task, however, may be debunking denial.

Debunking Denial

The previous five chapters of this book have outlined the denial arguments and provided some ammunition for refuting them. One of the best summaries of denial arguments and how they progress is provided by Michael Mann in his book on the hockey stick and climate wars:

1. CO2 is not actually increasing.

2. Even if it is, the increase has no impact on the climate since there is no convincing evidence of warming.

3. Even if there is warming, it is due to natural causes.

4. Even if the warming cannot be explained by natural causes, the human impact is small, and the impact of continued greenhouse gas emissions will be minor.

5. Even if the current and projected future human effects on Earth's climate are not negligible, the changes are generally going to be good for us.

6. Whether or not the changes are going to be good for us, humans are very adept at adapting to changes; besides, it's too late to do anything about it, and/or a technological fix is bound to come along when we really need it.[492]

Mann's listing of arguments outlines a series of stages, or a "ladder" that denial ideologues climb when the arguments at an earlier stage are debunked. You may find yourself in a discussion where someone starts climbing the ladder as you refute the lower stages—a kind of moving target that will be difficult to counter because your interlocutor does not want to agree with anything you say, period.

Ideology versus science, the theme with which we began, is the basic explanation of why it is so difficult to argue with denial ideologues. Many denial ideologues reach the highest stage of argument because they are convinced of the rightness of their position regardless of anything they hear or encounter. "When they deny global warming, then, conservatives think the best minds are actually on their side. They think they're the champions of truth and reality, and they're deeply attached to this view. That is why head-on attempts to persuade them otherwise usually fail."[493] What can one do with someone like this? Reiterating the science may work with some, but for most it will be necessary to see ideology for what it is: an intellectual failure to confront the facts. Ideologues and scientists talk past each other because the scientists are looking at facts and ideologues are blocking them out. Although we may not be able to change the minds of the Patrick Michaels or James Inhofes of the world, we may be able to surround them with people who can understand climate science and its implications for us. Most directly as a consequence of the arguments of climate scientists, we can make denial seem a dangerous fallacy. The denial ideologues will be forced to step back, out of the way, so that the rest of us can get on with the needed changes in energy and the economy. This will become increasingly possible with more frequent extreme weather.[494]

Debunking denial often depends on the social context of understanding climate change. Different regions of the country may have different views, shaped by the social milieu and educational perspectives of those regions. A Harvard Business School informal survey found regional differences: "In Northern California, 80% of the audience thought climate change was largely man-made and that urgent action to address it was both needed and realistic, while 20% believed it was a random fluctuation warranting no urgent action," says Lassiter, the Sen. John Heinz Professor of Management Practice in Environmental Management at Harvard Business School. "In Houston, it was the flip-flop, with 20% [believing climate change was largely man made and urgent action was needed]." We have seen how difficult it is to address climate change in Texas. Lassiter continues: "In New York, while nearly 100% thought climate change was man made, only half believed there was the political will—in the United States or abroad—to take urgent actions that would have a material impact on the problem."[495] Clearly, a message about climate change would be shaped differently for Texas and New York. Knowing the social context for debunking denial is essential.

You will need to be particularly wary of those who argue "man has dominion over nature." This argument, which seems to have biblical resonance, can be a kind of last resort for those who do not want to confront reality. The idea that we are somehow disconnected from nature is a particularly dangerous one. It implies that humans have no dependence on the ecosystem services provided by nature, including clean water and air as well as food and fiber. It provides denial ideologues with an excuse to ignore climate science and reaches its apotheosis in statements such as "man cannot destroy the earth, only God can." It feeds into the denial arguments such as "the earth is cooling," despite the evidence, and "CO2 has no relation to global temperature." Fossil fuel is considered an endless resource with no consequence for the fate of the earth, including humans as well as nature.

Albert Einstein beautifully expressed our need to overcome the danger of this mode of thinking. "A human being is part of the whole, which we call the Universe: a part limited in time and space. He experiences himself, his thoughts and feelings, as something separated from the rest, a kind of optical delusion of his consciousness. This delusion is a kind of prison for us, restricting us to our personal desires and affection for a few persons nearest us. Our task must be to free ourselves from this prison by widening our circle of compassion to embrace all living creatures and the whole of nature in its astonishing beauty."[496]

Why is it even necessary to debate with denial ideologues? As the surveys described in this book indicate, they are a minority of the population. This small group, however, can have a large effect on public opinion.[497] Survey research has consistently shown that most Americans do not agree with denial ideologues, but the ideologues nevertheless have inordinate influence on policy because of their fervency. The Republicans in Congress demonstrate this magnificently.

Beware of arguments that the government cannot, or should not, do anything about climate change. As Nobel laureate economists such as Joseph Stiglitz have argued, market failures are not temporary aberrations of capitalism that will self-correct with free markets. They are fundamental problems that only governments can solve. The energy market, in particular, is a highly volatile and error-prone market, subject to physical and natural constraints that have nothing to do with economic markets. Its future is very much wrapped up with the ideology and politics of climate change, and in turn our future is very much wrapped up in the energy market. Social change will be driven by the ways that governments regulate and shape the energy market, through subsidies, tax breaks, investments, and regulation.

Governments exercise, in most countries, jurisdiction over air pollutants. Citizens of nearly all persuasions will accept this, from conservative to liberal, libertarian to socialists, or whatever political label they choose. The devil is in the details, of course, because some people's pollutants are other people's jobs. The amount and source of pollutants can be points of major contention. In the case of climate change, however, there is an even more intractable problem: Is CO2 a pollutant? In the section on national politics in chapter 4, I reviewed the various arguments and cited the section of the Clean Air Act that mentions climate and defines pollutant. Nevertheless, denial ideologues continue to pursue this issue with a vengeance; for example, "In Western countries, including Australia and New Zealand, it is now widely believed that carbon dioxide is a dangerous pollutant whose level in the atmosphere needs to be controlled. This grotesque misconception did not arise by accident, but is the result of a skilful propaganda campaign mounted since the early 1990s by environmental lobby groups and their media and political supporters."[498]

Excluding the most important greenhouse gas from climate policy by definition is, of course, a rhetorical trick that is easily refuted with evidence. From Tyndall to Arrhenius, Revelle, Keeling, Hansen, and many other scientists, the role of CO2 has been substantiated again and again. To call this research "skillful propaganda" instead of science is semantic legerdemain with no relation to the facts. Because of this misrepresentation of science, government policies have been hamstrung.

Another problem of implementing climate policies is the absence of foresight on the problems of climate change. Nicholas Stern, who did research on the costs of climate change, notes that the crisis is much more gradual than others.[499] Because other crises seem to have higher priority, resources are diverted to resolving them first, and the more fundamental essentials of climate policies are disregarded. Stern and climate scientists point out that delays in reducing emissions will make eventual resolution increasingly costly. This is indeed a frightening prospect. Already total global economic production is only twice the annual cost of carbon emissions, but we have hardly begun to address these costs, and they will rapidly overtake all other costs if they are neglected. In other words, the costs of delay are mounting and will become so overwhelming that they will crowd out all other forms of investment.

Dealing with climate change will require a paradigm shift, away from the conventional ways of thinking about pollution: "the fact that overcoming global warming demands something qualitatively different from limiting our contamination of nature. It demands unleashing human power, creating a new economy, and remaking nature as we prepare for the future."[500] The EPA's enforcement of the Clean Air Act is thrown into question by this concept. If climate change cannot be countered solely with pollution regulations, society will have to transform its use of energy. "Economic development" must be viewed in a different way, involving a reorientation of energy production and use. What was previously regarded as something external, such as sulfur dioxide that could be easily removed by scrubbers, is now inherent in energy production on a massive scale. How can this change?

Fundamentally, this change will involve true-cost pricing of energy. At present, fossil fuel prices have a fatal flaw that underestimates the natural and social costs of their use. The infamous depletion allowance is the opposite of their true cost; by lowering the tax liability of producers, the government not only underprices this resource but also encourages faster depletion. In addition, all of the hidden health and environmental costs are left out. Both of these market failures are bringing environmental problems faster and more acutely to us. Until this is changed through regulation (don't count on the free market), climate change and other health problems will increase exponentially.

Perhaps the most effective refutation of denial is the slow, inexorable increase in temperatures. While observing the necessary caution about generalizing from daily weather, we can detect trends such as the heat records in 2012 and the increase in weather-related disasters during the first decade of the twenty-first century.[501] These events may not dissuade someone dedicated to denial ideology, but their accumulation will certainly sow doubts and eventually undermine its credibility.

Conclusion

Coming full circle, perhaps the most important personal action you can take is to become familiar with the issues and prospects for unavoidable lifestyle changes. Energy will never be as cheap and readily available as it has been. Not only travel, but also all of the other things in life that depend on energy and fossil fuels will be affected. Households will adapt with new building codes, appliance standards and travel modes following from strict energy regulation. Communities will change toward more localized production of energy and food. Nations will reorient their economic and political systems to account for the true costs of energy. International relations will involve higher levels of conflict, migration, and humanitarian disasters.

Among the most important choices made by individuals are consumption decisions, including those that involve different levels of energy use and efficiencies. How those decisions are made is the subject of social science research.[502] It is important to understand that using "status quo" assumptions for decision making is one of the major sources of increased greenhouse emissions. Gasoline-powered vehicles, coal-fired power plants (whose electricity rates are artificially low), and processed or imported foods are significant contributors to climate change, but very few consumers have the "sovereignty" to purchase alternatives. As I mentioned in the preface, inertia often has a lot to do with resolving the puzzle of why popular understanding of climate science lags so far behind the science, and inertia in consumer choices also has a lot to do with powerlessness in making decisions to address climate problems.

Another issue that has to be confronted in discussing climate change is understanding cause and effect. As the statements for and against treating carbon dioxide as a pollutant (in chapters 3 and 4) illustrate, people sometimes have difficulty with causes of climate change. It is particularly difficult for people to see how their minor role in consuming energy has any effect on global warming. We need a paradigm shift that leads people to see the whole context of energy use.

It may take some effort to convey the sense of urgency and gravity of the threat of climate change because of how remote it seems to most people. Nevertheless, it is an essential task of anyone who understands the urgency and gravity of the problem. As the International Energy Agency (IEA) has said, "After 2017, we will lose the chance to limit the temperature increase to 2 degrees Celsius."[503] That means that the decisions and actions we take in the next few years will determine the long-term health of the earth.

If greenhouse gas emissions follow the current trajectory, we will be on track for a 6°C increase in temperatures by 2100, which will create major disasters throughout the world. Reducing emissions immediately would put us on the lowest trajectory, while delaying until after 2020 would mean that controlling emissions sustainably would come at a much higher cost. As the IEA report notes, "Delaying action is a false economy: for every $1.00 of investment in cleaner technology that is avoided in the power sector before 2020, an additional $4.30 would need to be spent after 2020 to compensate for the increased emissions."[504] That's a rather pricey four-to-one ratio of future costs.

In this book, I have tried to convey urgency and gravity. Because people seem to avoid the issue, I have described some of the reasons individuals and society do not want to understand the urgency of climate change. Using this information to debunk the denial ideologues will help reverse this trend. Armed with that ammunition, it may be possible for you to promote climate science and support efforts to deal with the consequences of climate change.

Even if you are able to convince listeners of the urgency and gravity of the threat of climate change, you face another form of resistance: many people will deny a threat because they cannot deal emotionally with it. Since the consequences of climate change are so tremendous and at the same time so remote, many people accept the denial argument that there is no scientific basis for climate change because they find it too overwhelming to acknowledge the science. They simply don't want to hear anything about it. "Climate change presents numerous ideological challenges to our culture and our beliefs. People say, 'Wait a second, this is really going to affect how we live!' "[505]

Incredulity is a natural response to exasperation from the challenges posed by climate science. In addition to reinforcement of incredulity by denial ideology, there is a tendency to reject the science because of trepidation. "When scientists say we will cross tipping points leading to chaotic weather for centuries, we retreat to incredulity."[506] The "social trap" that some social scientists describe involves thinking about the problem in the abstract, as, for example, in a statement that "nothing I do will make a difference." Denial of climate science may play no role at first in this thinking, but once someone has accepted this nihilistic premise, denial may provide a rationale for avoiding the problem.

When consequences of climate change become severe, panic may set in and people will seek out quick solutions. Geoengineering is one such "silver bullet" that has been proposed by some; it may become necessary if denial ideology postpones needed action until it is deemed essential. But geoengineering is fraught with risks of unintended consequences. Parkinson describes unintended consequences that can affect the best intentions of proponents of geoengineering: "We should be able to do better than destroy other ecosystems in order to maintain our energy-consumptive lifestyles."[507] Her analysis covers a wide variety of geoengineering, including aerosols in the atmosphere, iron filings in the oceans, reflective covers in deserts, and some space-based systems. The unintended consequences of all of them are highly destructive.

Many commentators have noted that effective actions on climate change occur at the local and state level in the United States. These are commendable. But it will take action at the international level, enforced by national governments, to resolve global climate problems. No matter how many local or regional initiatives are successful, the effort requires that all cities and countries reduce emissions together; this is the epic challenge facing the world. As stated by David Orr, we have to try not to "evict ourselves from the only paradise we've ever known."[508]

The future can be precisely measured. At Copenhagen and Cancun, world leaders agreed to a 2°C increase in world temperature. Many scientists, including James Hansen and others, consider even this limit dangerous, but it can be taken as a "red line" for avoiding future climate disasters. As we approach this limit, more precise calculations can be made of the effects of greenhouse gas concentrations and the contributions of various kinds of emissions. Ratcheting down these emissions will have to be a major effort of all nations and peoples.

The question for our generation and future generations to answer is: Will we keep oil and coal in the ground? Who will decide, and who will benefit? Ultimately, it is an issue of intergenerational justice.[509] Climate scientists are becoming increasingly concerned about the intergenerational effects of global warming. The present generation bears enormous responsibility for actions that may put future generations in peril.

I am over 70 years old, and I may not see many of the consequences of climate change, but my children and grandchildren will. As one author has said, "We're not good at planning for our great-grandchildren, yet this is what is required of our generation and of those who follow us."[510]

One young woman, Abigail Borah of Middlebury College, spoke for her generation:

> I am speaking on behalf of the United States of America because my negotiators cannot. The obstructionist Congress has shackled justice and delayed ambition for far too long. I am scared for my future. [The year] 2020 is too late to wait. We need an urgent path to a fair, ambitious, and legally binding treaty. We need leaders who will commit to real change, not empty rhetoric. Keep your promises. Keep our hope alive.

She spoke to diplomats in Durban, South Africa, at the Conference of Parties of the UNFCCC, but she also spoke to the world. Denial ideology has stymied action not only in the United States, but also around the world. Will humanity realize the implications of climate science in time to act?

References

American Legislative Exchange Council. *EPA's Regulatory Train Wreck.* 2011. http://www.regulatorytrainwreck.com.

Alexander, Ralph B. *Global Warming False Alarm.* Royal Oak, MI: Canterbury Press, 2012.

Archer, David. *The Long Thaw: How Humans Are Changing the Next 100,000 Years of Earth's Climate (Science Essentials).* Princeton University Press. 2008. Kindle edition.

Ball, Jim. *Washington Fiddles While the Climate Burns, Yet Hope Remains.* http://www.huffingtonpost.com.

Banner, Bob, et al. *Sustainability.* Hopedance, 2008.

Beck, Glenn. *An Inconvenient Book.* Threshhold, 2007.

Bell, Larry. *Climate of Corruption.* Greanleaf, 2011.

Bonfiglio, Olga. *Some Sociological Explanations for Climate Change Denial.* 2011. http://www.opednews.com.

Booker, Christopher. *The Real Warming Disaster.* Continuum, 2009.

Bowen, Mark. *Censoring Science: Dr. James Hansen and the Truth of Global Warming*. Penguin Group, 2008.

Broder, John. "Climate Change Doubt Is Tea Party Article of Faith." *New York Times*, October 21, 2010.

Brown, Lester. *World on the Edge*. W. W. Norton, 2011.

Brulle, Robert, Jason Carmichael, and J. Jenkins. "Shifting Public Opinion on Climate Change: An Empirical Assessment of Factors Influencing Concern over Climate Change in the U.S., 2002–2010." *Climatic Change*, 2012.

Carter, Robert M. *Climate: The Counter Consensus*. Stacey International, 2010.

Center for the Study of CO2 and Global Change. *Climate Change Reconsidered*. 2011. http://www.nipccreport.org.

Cherson, Adam. *Political Ecologies*. Greencore Books, 2010.

Climate Central. *Global Weirdness: Severe Storms, Deadly Heat Waves, Relentless Drought, Rising Seas and the Weather of the Future*. Random House, 2012. Kindle edition.

Coll, Steve. *Private Empire: ExxonMobil and American Power*. Penguin Group, 2012. Kindle edition.

Conway, Erik, and Naomi Oreskes. *Merchants of Doubt*. Bloomsbury Press, 2010.

Cornwall Alliance. *Cornwall Alliance Releases An Evangelical Declaration on Global Warming*. 2011c. http://www.cornwallalliance. org/alert.

------. *Newsletter.* February 16, 2011 (2011b).

------. *Sounding the Alarm about Dangerous Environmental Extremism.* 2011a. http://www.cornwallalliance.org/alert/.

Costanza, Robert, Ralph d'Arge, Rudolf de Groot, Stephen Farber, Monica Grasso, Bruce Hannon, Karin Limburg, et al. "The Value of the World's Ecosystem Services and Natural Capital." *Nature* 387 (May 15, 1997), 253-260.

Cromwell, Ben. *Touch: Making Contact with Climate Change.* 2011. Kindle edition.

Cullen, Heidi. *The Weather of the Future.* Harper-Collins, 2010.

deBuys, William. *A Great Aridness: Climate Change and the Future of the American Southwest.* Oxford University Press, 2011. Kindle edition.

Diffenbaugh, Noah S., Thomas W. Hertel, Martin Scherer, and Monika Verma. "Response of Corn Markets to Climate Volatility under Alternative Energy Futures." *Nature Climate Change Letter*, April 22, 2012.

Dunlap, Riley E., and Aaron M. McCright. "Organized Climate-Change Denial." In *Oxford Handbook of Climate Change and Society.* Oxford University Press, 2011.

Edsall, Thomas Byrne. *The Age of Austerity: How Scarcity Will Remake American Politics.* Random House, 2012. Kindle edition.

Einstein, Albert. *Ideas and Opinions.* Three River Press, 1954.

Emanuel, Kerry. "What We Know about Climate Change." *Boston Review*, 2012.

Energy Information Administration. "Carbon Dioxide Emissions from Generation of Electric Power in the United States." Department of Energy. http://www.eia.doe.gov/cneaf/electricity/page/co2_report/co2report.html#electric.

Environmental Protection Agency. *eGrid.* 2010. http://www.epa.gov/cleanenergy/energy-resources/egrid/index.html.

Epstein, Paul. "Food Security and Climate Change: The True Cost of Carbon." *The Atlantic*, September 27, 2011.

Epstein, Paul, and Dan Ferber. *Changing Planet, Changing Health.* University of California Press, 2011.

Fagan, Brian. *The Great Warming: Climate Change and the Rise and Fall of Civilizations.* Bloomsbury Publishing Plc., 2010. Kindle edition.

Festinger, Leon, Henry Riecken, and Stanley Schachter. *When Prophecy Fails.* Pinter and Martin, 1956.

Festinger, Leon. *A Theory of Cognitive Dissonance.* Row, Peterson, 1957.

Foster, John Bellamy, Brett Clark, and Richard York. *The Ecological Rift.* Monthly Review Press, 2010.

Friel, Howard. *The Lomborg Deception.* Yale University, 2010.

Gardiner, Stephen. *A Perfect Moral Storm: The Ethical Tragedy of Climate Change (Environmental Ethics and Science Policy).* Oxford University Press, USA, 2011. Kindle edition.

Gilbert, Richard, and Anthony Perl. *Transport Revolutions: Moving People and Freight without Oil.* Perseus Books Group, 2010. Kindle edition.

Gilding, Paul. *The Great Disruption*. Bloomsbury Press, 2011.

Global Humanitarian Forum. *Climate Change: Human Impact Report, the Anatomy of a Silent Crisis*. 2009. http://www.ghg-ge.org.

Glover, Peter C., and Michael J. Economides. *Energy and Climate Wars*. Continuum Books, 2010.

Goreham, Steve. *The Mad, Mad, Mad World of Climatism*. New Lenox Books, 2012.

Greenpeace. *Dealing in Doubt*. Greenpeace USA, 2013.

Greer, John Michael. *The Eco-Technic Future*. New Society, 2009.

------. *The Long Descent*. New Society, 2008.

Gunther, Marc. *Suck It Up: How Capturing Carbon from the Air Can Help Solve the Climate Crisis*. 2012. Kindle edition.

Gurria, Angel. "Green Growth: Time to Reframe the Way We Think About Growth." IISD Reporting Services, March 9, 2011.

Hamilton, Clive. *Growth Fetish*. Allen and Unwin, 2003.

------. *Requiem for a Species: Why We Resist the Truth about Climate Change*. Earth Scan, 2010 (2010a).

------. "Why We Resist the Truth about Climate Change." A paper to the Climate Controversies: Science and Politics conference, Museum of Natural Sciences, Brussels, October 28, 2010 (2010b).

Hansen, James. *Michael Crichton's "Scientific Method."* Crichton_20050927.pdf.

------. *Storms of My Grandchildren*. Bloomsberry, 2009.

Hansen, James, Pushker Kharecha, Makiko Sato, Frank Ackerman, Paul Epstein, Paul J. Hearty, Ove Hoegh-Guldberg, et al. *The Case for Young People and Nature: A Path to a Healthy, Natural, Prosperous Future*. Cornell University Library, 2011.

Hansen, James, Makiko Satoa, and Reto Ruedyb. "Perception of Climate Change." Proceedings of the National Academy of Sciences. 2012. http://www.pnas.org/cgi/doi/10.1073/pnas.1205276109.

Hartmann, Thom. *The Last Hours of Ancient Sunlight*. Three Rivers, 2004.

Hertsgaard, Mark. "California Takes the Lead with New Climate Initiatives." 2012. http://www.e360.yale.edu.

------. *Hot: Living through the Next Fifty Years on Earth*. Houghton Mifflin Harcourt, 2011.

Heinberg, Richard. *The End of Growth: Adapting to Our New Economic Reality*. Perseus Books Group, 2011. Kindle edition.

------. *The Party's Over*. New Society, 2005.

Helm, Dieter. *The Carbon Crunch*. Yale University, 2012. Kindle edition.

Hewitt, William F. *A Newer World, Politics Money, Technology, and What's Really Being Done to Solve the Climate Crisis*. University of New Hampshire Press, 2013.

Hoggan, James. *Climate Cover-Up*. Greystone Books, 2009.

------. "On Twisting Words and Dodging Responsibility." August 18, 2006. http://www.desmogblog.com.

Holmgren, David. *Future Scenarios*. Green Press, 2008.

Humes, Edward. *Force of Nature: The Unlikely Story of Wal-Mart's Green Revolution*. HarperBusiness, 2010.

Inhofe, Senator James. *The Greatest Hoax: How the Global Warming Conspiracy Threatens Your Future*. Midpoint Trade Books, 2012. Kindle edition.

Intergovernmental Panel on Climate Change. *Climate Change 2001: Synthesis Report*. 2001. http://www.ipcc.ch.

------. *Fourth Assessment Report*. 2007. http://www.ipcc.ch.

------. *Fifth Assessment Report*. 2013. http://www.ipcc.ch.

International Energy Agency. Presentation to the Press. 2011. http://www.iea.org/weo/.

Johnson, Brad. "Montana Legislator Who Introduced Bill to Declare Global Warming 'Natural.' " 2011. http://www.thinkprogress.org.

Jolis, Anne. "The Weather Isn't Getting Weirder." *Wall Street Journal*, February 10, 2011.

Kabaservice, Goeffrey. *Rule and Ruin*. Oxford University Press, 2012.

Kahan, Dan, et al. *The Tragedy of the Risk-Perception Commons: Culture Conflict, Rationality Conflict, and Climate Change*. Yale University, 2011.

Kintisch, Eli. *Hack the Planet*. John Wiley and Sons, 2010.

Klare, Michael. *Rising Powers, Shrinking Planet.* Henry Holt, 2008.

Koerth-Baker, Maggie. *Before the Lights Go Out.* John Wiley and Sons, 2012.

Kraemer, Susan. "Another Big Win for Koch Tea Party Funding—New Hampshire Abandons its RGGI Polluter Controls." http://www.cleantechnica.com.

Larkin, Amy. *Environmental Debt.* Palgrave/Macmillan, 2013.

Leiserowitz, A., E. Maibach, C. Roser-Renouf, and J. D. Hmielowski. "Politics and Global Warming: Democrats, Republicans, Independents, and the Tea Party." Yale University and George Mason University. New Haven, CT: Yale Project on Climate Change Communication, 2011.

Leiserowitz, A., E. Maibach, C. Roser-Renouf, and N. Smith. "Climate Change in the American Mind: Americans' Global Warming Beliefs and Attitudes in May 2011." Yale University and George Mason University, 2011.

Leiserowitz, A., N. Smith, and J. R. Marlon. "American Teens' Knowledge of Climate Change." Yale University. New Haven, CT: Yale Project on Climate Change Communication, 2011. http://environment.yale.edu/uploads/american-teens-knowledge-of-climate-change.pdf.

Leiserowitz, A., E. Maibach, C. Roser-Renouf, and J. D. Hmielowski. "Extreme Weather, Climate and Preparedness in the American Mind." Yale University and George Mason University. New Haven, CT: Yale Project on Climate Change Communication, 2012.

Leiserowitz, A., E. Maibach, C. Roser-Renouf, and N. Smith. "Global Warming's Six Americas, September 2012." Yale University and George

Mason University. New Haven, CT: Yale Project on Climate Change Communication, 2012.

Lever- Tracy, Constance. *Confronting Climate Change*. Taylor and Francis, 2011. Kindle edition.

Lewandowsky, Stephan. "Climate Sceptic Science." http://www.abc. net.au.

Linden, Eugene. "Betting the Farm against Climate Change." *Los Angeles Times*, August 28, 2011.

Lomborg, Bjorn. *Cool It!* Random House, 2007.

Lovins, Amory. *Reinventing Fire: Bold Business Solutions for the New Energy Era*. Chelsea Green Publishing, 2011. Kindle edition.

Lovins, L. Hunter, and Boyd Cohen. *Climate Capitalism*. Hill and Wang, 2011.

Lynas, Mark. *High Tide: How Climate Crisis is Engulfing Our Planet.* Harper Collins, 2010. Kindle edition.

Mann, Michael. *The Hockey Stick and the Climate Wars: Dispatches from the Front Lines*. Perseus Books Group, 2012. Kindle edition.

Marsden, William. *Fools Rule: Inside the Failed Politics of Climate Change*. Alfred A. Knopf Canada, 2011.

Martenson, Chris. *The Crash Course: The Unsustainable Future of Our Economy, Energy, and Environment*. John Wiley and Sons, 2011.

Maibach, Edward, Kristopher Wilson, and James Witte. "A National Survey of Television Meteorologists about Climate

Change." George Mason University Center for Climate Change Communication, 2010.

Mayer, Jane. "Covert Operations." *New Yorker*, August 31, 2010.

McCright, Aaron M., and Riley E. Dunlap. "The Politicization of Climate Change and Polarization in the American Public's Views of Global Warming, 2001–2010." *Sociological Quarterly* 52, no. 2 (Spring 2011), pages 155–194.

McKibben, Bill. *Deep Economy*. Henry Holt, 2007.

------. "My life as a communist." *Washington Post*. March 1, 2011. http://www.washingtonpost.com.

------. *Eaarth*. Henry Holt, 2010.

------. *The Global Warming Reader*. OR Books, 2011. Kindle edition.

McKibben, Bill, Miller, Asher; Heinberg, Richard; Erika, Allen; David, Orr; Stephanie, Mills; Sandra, Postel; Peter, Whybrow; Gloria, Flora; Daniel, Lerch. *The Post Carbon Reader: Managing the 21st Century's Sustainability Crises*. Watershed Media in collaboration with Post Carbon Institute, 2011. Kindle edition.

McMichael, Phillip. "The World Food Crisis in Historical Perspective." *Monthly Review*, July–August 2009.

McPherson, William. *Climate Change is a Plot Invented by a Bunch of Hippies*. 2013. Kindle edition.

------. *Extreme Weather and Extreme Denial*. 2012. Kindle edition.

------. *Ideology and Change*. National Press Books, 1973.

Meadows, Donella, Dennis Meadows, and Jorgen Randers. *Limits to Growth*. Chelsea Green, 2004.

Mearns, Robin, and Andrew Norton. *Social Dimensions of Climate Change*. World Bank, 2010.

Meckler, Mark, and Jenny Beth Martin. *Tea Party Patriots: The Second American Revolution*. Macmillan, 2012. Kindle edition.

Michaels, David. *Doubt Is Their Product: How Industry's Assault on Science Threatens Your Health*. Oxford University Press, 2008.

Michaels, Patrick. *Meltdown*. Cato Institute, 2004.

------. Testimony, House Committee on Small Business, 1998. http://www.cato.org.

Michaels, Patrick, and Robert Balling. *Climate of Extremes*. Cato Institute, 2009.

Montford, A. W. *Hockey Stick Illusion*. Stacey International, 2010.

Mooney, Chris. *The Republican Brain: The Science of Why They Deny Science—and Reality*. John Wiley and Sons, 2012. Kindle edition.

------. *The Republican War on Science*. Basic Books, 2006.

------. "The Science of Why We Don't Believe Science." *Mother Jones*, April 18, 2011.

------. *Storm World*. Harcourt, 2007.

------. "Why Conservatives Deny Global Warming." http://www.huffingtonpost.com, March 26, 2012.

Mooney, Chris, and Sheril Kirshenbaum. *Unscientific America*. Basic Books, 2010.

Moser, Susanne C., and Lisa Dilling. *Creating a Climate for Change: Communicating Climate Change and Facilitating Social Change.* 2007. Kindle edition.

Musser, Mark. "The Nazi Origins of Apocalyptic Global Warming Theory." *American Thinker*, February 23, 2011.

National Academy of Science. "Expert Credibility in Climate Change." Proceedings of the National Academy of Science, July 6, 2010.

National Aeronautics and Space Administration. "What Makes Scientists Think That Humans Are Causing Global Warming Now?" 2010. http://www.earthobservatory.nasa.gov.

National Center for Atmospheric Research. "Record High Temperatures Far Outpace Record Lows Across U.S." *NCAR AtmosNews*, November 12, 2009. http://www.ucar.edu.

Negin, Elliot. "ALEC's Other 'Deadly Force' Campaign to Kill Climate Initiatives." April 20, 2012. http://www.huffingtonpost.com.

Non-Governmental International Panel on Climate Change. "Climate Change Reconsidered" Heartland Institute, 2009.

Non-Governmental International Panel on Climate Change. "Climate Change Reconsidered: 2011 Interim Report." Heartland Institute, 2011.

Non-Governmental International Panel on Climate Change. "Climate Change Reconsidered II, Summary for Policymakers." Heartland Institute, 2013.

National Oceanic and Atmospheric Administration. "State of the Climate Global Analysis Annual 2010." http://www.ncdc.noaa.gov/sotc/global/.

Nordhaus, William. "Why the Global Warming Skeptics Are Wrong." *New York Review of Books*, March 22, 2012.

Norgaard, Kari Marie. *Living in Denial: Climate Change, Emotions, and Everyday Life*. 2011. Kindle edition.

National Research Council. "Stabilization Targets for Atmospheric Greenhouse Gas Concentrations." National Academy of Sciences, 2010.

Oppenheimer, Robert. *Climate Change Debunked*. CreateSpace, 2010.

Oreskes, Naomi, and Erik Conway. *art*. Bloomsbury Press, 2010.

Orr, David. *Down to the Wire*. Oxford University Press, 2009.

Otto, Shawn Lawrence. *Fool Me Twice: Fighting the Assault on Science in America*. Rodale, 2011. Kindle edition.

Parenti, Chistian. *Tropic of Chaos*. Nation Books, 2011.

Parkinson, Claire. *Coming Climate Crisis? Consider the Past, Beware the Big Fix*." Rowman and Littlefield, 2010. Kindle edition.

Perry, Rick. *Fed Up! Our Fight to Save America from Washington*. Little, Brown, 2010.

Pew Research Center. "Wide Partisan Divide over Global Warming." October 27, 2010.

Pielke, Roger. "A Positive Path for Meeting the Global Climate Challenge." http://www.e360.yale.edu.

Pooley, Eric. *Climate War*. Hyperion, 2009.

Popper, Karl. *The Logic of Scientific Discovery*. Routledge Classics, 2002.

Randers, Jorgen. *2052: A Global Forecast for the Next Forty Years*. Chelsea Green Publishing, 2012. Kindle edition.

Restuccia, Andrew. "Environmentalists Targeting Upton in New Advertisements." *The Hill*, February 28, 2011.

Revkin, Andrew. "In Climate Fight, Tracking the Line between Diagnosis and Treatment." *New York Times*, February 1, 2012.

Rich, Frank. "Why Wouldn't the Tea Party Shut It Down?" *New York Times*, February 27, 2011.

Richter, Burton. *Beyond Smoke and Mirrors*. Cambridge University Press, 2010.

Rigg, Kelly. "Climate Change and Extreme Weather." September 5, 2011. http://www.huffingtonpost.com.

Rogers, Heather. *Green Gone Wrong*. Simon and Schuster, 2010.

Rosenthal, Elizabeth. "Doubts about Climate Change." *New York Times*, May 25, 2010.

Rothkopf, David. *Power, Inc.: The Epic Rivalry between Big Business and Government—and the Reckoning That Lies Ahead*. Macmillan, 2012. Kindle edition.

Rubin, Jeff. *Why Your World is About to Get a Lot Smaller*. Random House, 2008.

Shellenberger, Michael, and Ted Nordhaus. *Break Through: From the Death of Environmentalism to the Politics of Possibility*. 2007. Kindle edition.

Schneider, Stephen. "Science as a Contact Sport." National Geographic Society, 2009.

Skocpol, Theda, and Vanessa Williamson. *The Tea Party and the Remaking of Republican Conservatism*. Oxford University Press, 2011. Kindle edition.

Shearman, David, and Joseph Wayne Smith. *The Climate Change Challenge and the Failure of Democracy*. Praeger, 2007.

Shellenberger, Michael, and Ted Nordhaus, eds. *Love Your Monsters*. Breakthrough Institute, 2012.

Sherwin, Elton. *Addicted to Energy*. Energy House Publishing, 2011.

Sierra Club. *Global Warming and Ozone Depletion*. 2010. http://www.sierraclub.org.

Spencer, Roy. *The Great Global Warming Blunder*. Encounter Books, 2009.

Spooner, John, and Bob Carter. *Taxing Air*. Kelpie Press, 2013. Kindle edition.

Steiner, Christopher. *$20 a Gallon Gasoline*. Grand Central, 2009.

Stern, Nicholas. *The Global Deal*. Public Affairs, 2009. Kindle edition.

------. Stern Review on the economics of climate change. 2006. http://www.hm-treasury.gov.uk.

Sussman, Brian. *Climategate*. WorldNetDaily Books, 2010.

------. "Was 2010 the Hottest Year Ever?" *Human Events*, January 27, 2011.

Taylor, Ron. *Agenda 21: An Expose of the United Nations' Sustainable Development Initiative and the Forfeiture of American Sovereignty and Liberties*. 2010. Kindle edition.

Thiel, Stefan. "A Green Retreat." *Newsweek*, July 1, 2010.

University of Michigan. "Climate Compared: Public Opinion on Climate Change in the United States and Canada." 2011. http://www.closup.umich.edu/policy-reports.

Victor, David G *Global Warming Gridloc.,* Cambridge, 2011.

Ward, Peter. *The Flooded Earth*. Basic Books, 2010.

Watkiss, Paul. *The Impacts and Costs of Climate Change*. Oxford, UK: UNT Digital Library, 2005.

World Meteorological Organization. "2001-2012, A Decade of Climate Extremes." Press release no. 976.

Worldwatch Institute. *State of the World 2013*. Island Press, 2013.

Yacobucci, Brent D., John Blodgett, and Larry Parker. "U.S. Global Climate Change Policy: Evolving Views on Cost, Competitiveness, and Comprehensiveness—CRS Report." Congressional Research Service, 2011. Kindle edition.

Yergin, Daniel. "America's New Energy Policy." *New York Times*, June 10, 2012.

------. *The Quest*. Penguin Press, 2011.

Zaitchik, Alexander. *Common Nonsense*. John Wiley and Sons, 2010.

Endnotes

1. Thiel, 2010.
2. Rosenthal, 2010, Pew Research Center, 2010.
3. *Washington Post*, April 22, 2013.
4. ec.europa.eu/public_opinion, October 2011.
5. University of Michigan, 2011.
6. *Irish Times*, March 26, 2012.
7. Rosenthal, 2010.
8. Lieserowitz, Smith, and Marlon, 2011.
9. Moser and Dilling, 2007.
10. Norgaard, 2011.
11. Mooney and Kirshenbaum, 2010.
12. *Guardian*, March 30, 2012.
13. Popper, 2002.
14. IPCC, 2007.
15. IPCC, 2013.
16. Ibid.
17. Michaels and Balling, 2009.
18. *New Scientist*, November 2006.
19. *New York Times*, February 23, 2011.
20. Bloomberg News, August 22, 2011.
21. *New York Times*, June 30, 2010.
22. *Forbes*, May 19, 2013.
23. *Wall Street Journal*, October 21, 2011.
24. CBSnews.com, December 2, 2011.

25. Mann, 2012.
26. Hansen, 2009.
27. Hansen, 2009.
28. NBC, January 27, 2012.
29. McKibben, 2012.
30. *Washington Post*, March 2, 2013.
31. NRC, 2010.
32. Ibid.
33. Spooner and Carter, 2013.
34. NIPCC, 2013.
35. Ibid.
36. IPCC, 2007; Hansen, 2009; NRC, 2010.
37. *New York Times*, January 11, 2013.
38. McPherson, 2012.
39. Climate Central, 2012.
40. Guardian.co.uk, October 13, 2012.
41. NASA, 2010.
42. Marshall Shepherd, TEDx May 29, 2013.
43. Cullen, 2010.
44. Cullen, 2010.
45. Cullen, 2010.
46. Mooney and Kirshenbaum, 2010.
47. Maibach, Wilson, and Witte, 2010.
48. Mediamatters.org, July 15, 2012.
49. Maibach, Wilson, and Witte, 2010.
50. Huffingtonpost.com, January 30, 2012.
51. Spencer, 2010.
52. Ibid.
53. Ibid.
54. Spooner and Carter, 2013.
55. Hansen et al., 2012.
56. Moser and Dilling, 2007.
57. NASA, 2010.
58. Sussman, 2010.

59. NOAA, 2010.
60. WMO, 2013.
61. *Popular Science*, June 21, 2012.
62. Inofe, 2012.
63. Lever-Tracy, 2011.
64. For example, Sussman, 2010, Inhofe, 2012.
65. Cullen, 2010.
66. Reuters, June 13, 2011.
67. *New York Times*, May 14, 2013.
68. Norgaard, 2011.
69. Orr, 2009.
70. Otto, 2011.
71. Stern, 2009.
72. *Scientific American*, May 8, 2013.
73. IPCC, 2001.
74. Montford, 2010.
75. Mann, 2012.
76. Michaels, 2008.
77. Michaels, 1998.
78. Hansen, 2005.
79. Hoggan, 2009.
80. Mooney and Kirshenbaum, 2010.
81. Hansen, 2009.
82. Schneider, 2009.
83. Testimony of Patrick J. Michaels to the Subcommittee on Energy and Environment, Committee on Science and Technology, US House of Representatives, November 17, 2010.
84. Climate Progress, November 18, 2010.
85. Mayer, 2010.
86. Mayer, 2010.
87. http://nation.foxnews.com/global-warming/2012/04/01/study-refutes-manmade-warming#ixzz1qtX10jLC.
88. http://asnews.syr.edu/newsevents_2012/releases/ikaite_crystals_climate_STATEMENT.html, March 24, 2012.

89. Archer, 2008.
90. Alexander, 2012.
91. Mooney and Kirshenbaum, 2010.
92. Spencer, 2009.
93. Rushlimbaugh.com, June 10, 2011.
94. Beck, 2007.
95. Zaitchik, 2010.
96. Musser, 2011.
97. Musser, 2011.
98. *Tulsa World*, July 22, 2006.
99. Oppenheimer, 2010.
100. Statement of the Board of Directors of the American Association for the Advancement of Science Regarding Personal Attacks on Climate Scientists, Approved by the AAAS Board of Directors, June 28, 2011.
101. Sussman, 2011.
102. For example, Michaels, 2004; Bell, 2011.
103. Bowen, 2008.
104. NOAA, 2010.
105. Bell, 2011.
106. Archer, 2008.
107. *Nature*, April 5, 2012.
108. NIPCC, 2009.
109. NIPCC, 2009.
110. NIPCC, 2013.
111. NRC, 2010.
112. Bowen, 2008.
113. Emanuel, 2012.
114. Koerth-Baker, 2012.
115. deBuys, 2011.
116. *Nature*, July 28, 2011.
117. CSCDGC, 2011.
118. Cullen, 2010.
119. IPCC, 2007; Hansen, 2009.

120. *New York Times*, May 5, 2011.

121. IPCC, 2007.

122. ABCnews.go.com, March 23, 2008.

123. *Investor Business Daily*, November 25, 2011.

124. Glover and Economides, 2010.

125. Ibid.

126. Bowen, 2008.

127. PBS.org, September 18, 2012.

128. Ibid.

129. Ibid.

130. Festinger et al., 1956.

131. Festinger, 1957.

132. McPherson, 1973.

133. Norgaard, 2011; emphasis in original.

134. Norgaard, 2011.

135. Lynas, 2010.

136. Brulle, Carmichael, and Jenkins, 2012.

137. Ibid.

138. Pooley, 2009.

139. McPherson, 1973.

140. Goreham, 2012.

141. ABC News, April 15, 2010.

142. Broder, 2010.

143. Leiserowitz, Maibach, Roser-Renouf, and Hmielowski, 2011.

144. Ibid.

145. Ibid.

146. Ibid.

147. Skocpol and Williamson, 2011.

148. Meckler and Martin, 2012.

149. Skocpol and Williamson, 2011.

150. McPherson, 1973.

151. Inhofe, 2012.

152. *New York Times*, July 18, 2012.

153. *New York Times*, February 3, 2012.

154. Insideclimatenews.org, May 11, 2012.

155. *New York Times*, December 17, 2011.

156. Cornwall Alliance, 2011b.

157. Ibid.

158. Hamilton, 2003.

159. Cornwall Alliance Newsletter, June 29, 2011.

160. Cornwall Alliance Newsletter, May 30, 2012.

161. Cornwall Alliance Newsletter, July 17, 2013.

162. An Evangelical Declaration on Global Warming.

163. IPCC, 2001; IPCC, 2007; Hansen, 2011; Mann, 2012.

164. An Evangelical Declaration on Global Warming.

165. Ibid.

166. Cornwall Alliance Newsletter, March 23, 2011.

167. Cornwall Alliance, 2011a.

168. *Christian Post*, October 20, 2013.

169. Heartland Institute, 2010.

170. *Nature*, July 28, 2011.

171. Lieserowitz et al., 2012.

172. *Nation*, November 28, 2011.

173. KUOW Radio, May 9, 2012.

174. Desmogblog, May 23, 2012.

175. *Washington Examiner*, May 21, 2012.

176. Heartland Institute press release, May 2012.

177. http://climateaudit.org/2012/05/04/mckitrick-letter-to-heartland/, May 4, 2012.

178. *Los Angeles Times*, January 16, 2012.

179. Scienceblogs.com, February 20, 2012.

180. *Washington Post*, February 15, 2012.

181. ThinkProgress.org, February 14, 2012; emphasis in original.

182. NIPCC, 2011.

183. Desmogblog.com, February 14, 2012.

184. Politico.com, February 24, 2012.

185. Open letter, February 20, 2012.

186. http://act.engagementlab.org/sign/Climate_Storyshare_Petition/.

187. http://green.autoblog.com, March 5, 2012.

188. *Houston Chronicle*, February 29, 2012.

189. *Christian Science Monitor*, February 16, 2012.

190. Greenpeace, 2013.

191. Americans for Prosperity, 2010.

192. Mayer, 2010.

193. Ibid.

194. Pew Research Center, 2010.

195. Rich, 2011.

196. Grist.org, March 10, 2011.

197. *The Hill*, March 29, 2011.

198. Andrew Hoffman, University of Michigan, *New York Times*, April 9, 2011.

199. Mooney, 2011.

200. *Washington Post*, September 7, 2011.

201. *NPR Science Friday*, May 4, 2012.

202. McPherson, 1973.

203. McPherson, 2012.

204. *Human Events*, April 21, 2011.

205. McKibben et al., 2011.

206. Stern, 2009.

207. Bell, 2011; Booker, 2009; Carter, 2011; Michaels and Balling, 2009.

208. Cornwall Alliance Newsletter, April 11, 2012.

209. Festinger et al., 1956, 1957.

210. Lomborg, 2007.

211. Cornwall Alliance, 2011c.

212. *New York Times*, November 16, 2010.

213. *Rockford (IL) Register Star*, March 10, 2012.

214. Huffington Post, July 12, 2013.

215. *The Exponent*, Purdue University, August 26, 2013.

216. Cornwall Alliance, 2011c.

217. Cornwall Alliance Newsletter, June 8, 2011.

218. Ibid.

219. Ibid.
220. Cornwall Alliance Newsletter, January 18, 2012.
221. NPR, March 2, 2012.
222. Hansen, 2009.
223. Stern, 2009.
224. Mearns and Norton, 2010.
225. Brown, 2011.
226. Quoted in *BBC News*, February 25, 2011.
227. Spencer, 2010.
228. Global Humanitarian Forum, 2009.
229. Gardiner, 2011.
230. Yacobucci et al., 2011.
231. Meadows et al., 2004.
232. *New York Times*, January 16, 2013.
233. Bill McKibben, *Guardian*, February 7, 2012.
234. Randers, 2012.
235. deBuys, 2011.
236. Cf. Mann, 2012.
237. Gary Yohe, Wesleyan University, quoted by Revkin, 2012.
238. German Institute for Economic Research, 2005.
239. Stern, 2009.
240. Pielke, 2010.
241. Diamond, 2011.
242. Martenson, 2011.
243. Archer, 2008.
244. Rubin, 2008.
245. Klare, 2008.
246. Brune, 2011.
247. Lovins and Cohen, 2011.
248. Hartmann, 2004.
249. IAE press release, April 21, 2011.
250. Heinberg, 2011.
251. Sherwin, 2011.
252. *New York Times*, October 31, 2011.

253. Ibid.

254. .

255. Stern, 2009.

256. Heinberg, 2011.

257. Hertsgard, 2011; Lovins and Cohen, 2011.

258. Shearman and Smith, 2007; Holmgren, 2008, Gilding, 2011.

259. Bell, 2010.

260. Glover and Economides, 2010.

261. *Nation*, November 28, 2011.

262. Sherwin, 2011.

263. Lovins, 2011.

264. *Wall Street Journal*, 2011.

265. For example, NRC 2010, see chapter 1.

266. Thinkprogress.org, January 30, 2012.

267. *Wall Street Journal*, January 27, 2012.

268. *Science*, May 14, 2010. Emphasis in original.

269. *Wall Street Journal*, January 27, 2012.

270. Motherjones.com, January 13, 2012.

271. Taylor, 2010.

272. Inhofe, 2012.

273. *Nature*, May 27, 2012.

274. Stern, 2006.

275. Thinkprogress.org, March 8, 2012.

276. Global Humanitarian Forum, 2009; Martenson, 2011.

277. Nordhaus, 2012.

278. Stern, 2009.

279. Lovins and Cohen, 2011.

280. Costanza et al., 1997.

281. Lovins and Cohen, 2011.

282. Martenson, 2011.

283. Foster et al., 2010.

284. Rothkopf, 2012.

285. Dailycaller.com, February 24, 2011.

286. Ibid.

287. *New York Times*, June 4, 2012.

288. Ihinkprogress.org, February 17, 2011.

289. *Tampa Bay Times*, May 15, 2011.

290. American Legislative Exchange Council 2011.

291. American Legislative Exchange Council, 2011.

292. Hewitt, 2013.

293. International Monetary Fund Policy Paper, January 23, 2013.

294. *New York Times*, April 21, 2012.

295. Negin, 2012.

296. Sustainablebusiness.com, March 17, 2011.

297. Negin, 2012.

298. *Houston Chronicle*, February 17, 2010.

299. *New York Times*, February 28, 2013.

300. *Guardian*, October 7, 2009.

301. *Houston Chronicle*, October 10, 2011.

302. North Carolina Legislature, H 819; emphasis added.

303. North Carolina S.B. 171.

304. *BBC News*, June 5, 2012.

305. Utah H.J.R. 12.

306. Cromwell, 2012.

307. *Roanoke Times*, January 13, 2012.

308. AP, March 2, 2012.

309. *Wall Street Journal*, March 12, 2012.

310. Oklahoma Senate Bill 1742.

311. Oklahoma House Bill 1551.

312. NCSE, quoted in *New Jersey Star-Ledger*, February 17, 2012.

313. *Wall Street Journal*, March 12, 2012.

314. *Science*, August 5, 2011.

315. Otto, 2011.

316. Ibid.

317. Thinkprogress.org, April 12, 2013.

318. Minnesota Public Radio, March 17, 2008.

319. Seattlepi.com, June 12, 2011.

320. CBS News, August 29, 2011.

321. *New York Times*, September 8, 2011.

322. *Guardian*, August 12, 2011.

323. CBN News, August 5, 2011.

324. Perry, 2010.

325. Ibid.

326. *New York Post*, August 18, 2011.

327. *New York Times*, August 17, 2011.

328. *Washington Post*, August 18, 2011.

329. Fox News, August 25, 2011.

330. *Los Angeles Times*, September 30, 2011.

331. *New York Times*, September 8, 2011.

332. *Guardian*, January 4, 2012.

333. Mooney, 2006.

334. *Guardian*, January 4, 2012.

335. Vermont Public Radio, February 10, 2012.

336. Thinkprogress.org, February 10, 2012.

337. Ibid.

338. Business Green, January 9, 2012.

339. Ibid.

340. Politico, March 29, 2011.

341. *Iowa Independent*, April 5, 2011.

342. Politico, May 13, 2011.

343. *Macon Telegraph*, May 14, 2011.

344. Ibid.

345. *Boston Globe*, November 8, 2005.

346. The Commonwealth of Massachusetts Executive Department press release, December 7, 2005.

347. *The Moderate Voice*, September 4, 2012.

348. Reuters, September 5, 2012.

349. Romney spokeswoman Andrea Saul, May 18, 2011. Associated Press, May 27, 2011.

350. Politico.com, July 20, 2011.

351. Politico, July 18, 2011.

352. Mittromney.com/issues/energy.

353. *Chicago Tribune*, April 26, 2012.

354. USCA Case 09-1322, Document 1380690, June 26, 2012.

355. Oreskes and Conway, 2010.

356. Cited by Hoggan, 2006.

357. *Washington Times*, May 17, 2011.

358. NOAA, 2010.

359. *San Antonio Express*, October 7, 2013.

360. Source: Lieserowitz et al., 2011.

361. Ball, 2012.

362. Stern, 2009.

363. *New York Times*, January 21, 2013.

364. *New Yorker*, June 2012.

365. *Seattle Times*, February 18, 2012.

366. *The Hill*, September 26, 2011.

367. *Dallas Morning News*, September 26, 2011.

368. Inhofe, 2012.

369. Allvoices.com, May 21, 2013.

370. Mooney, 2006.

371. Orr, 2009.

372. *Washington Post*, September 22, 2011.

373. McCright and Dunlap, 2011.

374. Hamilton, 2010a.

375. *New York Times*, October 16, 2011.

376. Kabaservice, 2011.

377. Norgaard, 2011.

378. *Guardian*, February 19, 2012.

379. Statistics of the Presidential and Congressional Election of November 6, 2012, House Clerk.

380. Thinkprogress.org, June 26, 2013.

381. *National Journal*, May 9, 2013.

382. Ibid.

383. *Cleveland Plain Dealer*, March 2, 2011.

384. *Atlanta Journal-Constitution*, March 10, 2011.

385. Charles Bayless, retired president of WVU Tech and former CEO of two power companies, quoted in publicnewsservice.org.

386. *Bloomberg News*, March 1, 2011.

387. Otto, 2011.

388. Lovins and Cohen, 2011.

389. CSPAN, July 25, 2013.

390. *Washington Post*, May 20, 2013.

391. Environment and Public Works Committee, March 2, 2011.

392. Conway and Oreskes, 2010.

393. Fuelfix.com, February 24, 2012.

394. *Wall Street Journal*, March 15, 2011.

395. *New York Times*, March 8, 2011.

396. *Saint Petersburg Times*, March 14, 2011.

397. CBS News, March 16, 2011.

398. *Forbes*, October 14, 2011

399. *Plastics News*, March 7, 2011.

400. *Grist*, April 1, 2011.

401. Climate Depot, October 20, 2011.

402. Politico, April 5, 2011.

403. Science.house.gov, June 22, 2011.

404. *Washington Post*, November 21, 2011.

405. *Forbes*, February 24, 2013.

406. *The Hill*, May 9, 2012.

407. CBS News, December 2, 2011.

408. Bloomberg News, September 1, 2011.

409. Bloomberg News, July 18, 2013.

410. Ibid.

411. Portfolio.com, March 1, 2011.

412. *Colorado Independent*, March 28, 2012.

413. Heritage Foundation, March 30, 2011.

414. *Atlanta Journal-Constitution*, March 10, 2011; Lovins and Cohen, 2011.

415. Lovins and Cohen, 2011.

416. http://www.phys.org/news/2013-04-businesses-climate-law.html.

417. Larkin, 2013.
418. Humes, 2010.
419. Ibid.
420. Foster et al., 2010.
421. Letter from Secretary Steven Chu to Energy Department employees announcing his decision not to serve a second term, February 1, 2013.
422. Linden, 2011.
423. *Seattle Times*, September 17, 2013.
424. Moser and Dilling, 2007.
425. *Wall Street Journal*, April 15, 2011.
426. Energy Information Administration, 2000.
427. EPA, 2010.
428. http://ghgdata.epa.gov/ghgp/main.do.
429. NRC, 2010.
430. *Weekly Standard*, March 29, 2011.
431. *USA Today*, May 30, 2013.
432. Ibid.
433. *Lovins and Cohen, 2011.*
434. Ibid.
435. NIPCC, 2011.
436. Epstein and Ferber, 2011.
437. who.int/mediacentre/factsheets/fs266/en/index.html.
438. Epstein, 2011.
439. Reuters, October 24, 2011.
440. Bruce Campbell, Consortium of International Agricultural Research Centers, May 2012.
441. Thinkprogress.org, February 16, 2012; *emphasis in original*
442. Redorbit.com, May 7, 2012.
443. *Coll, 2012.*
444. Ibid.
445. Ibid.
446. Ibid.
447. ExxonMobil.com, May 16, 2012.

448. Greenpeace, 2013.

449. *Popular Science*, June 21, 2012.

450. Triplepundit.com, June 28, 2012.

451. MSNBC, June 29, 2012.

452. *deBuys, 2011.*

453. *For example, Stern, 2009; Friel, 2010.*

454. Worldwatch Institute, 2013.

455. Diffenbaugh et al., 2012.

456. *McPherson, 2012.*

457. *Stanford Report*, April 23, 2012.

458. *Slate*, July 16, 2013.

459. *New York Times*, October 14, 2009.

460. Whitehouse.gov, July 18, 2012.

461. Iowa State University Extension Service, December 2011.

462. Union of Concerned Scientists, March 10, 2011.

463. NRC, 2010.

464. EPA.gov, September 28, 2011.

465. Senate Committee on Environment and Public Works, http://www.epw.senate.gov, September 28, 2011.

466. Reuters, June 26, 2012.

467. Ibid.

468. Lovins and Cohen, 2011.

469. *Washington Post*, September 28, 2011.

470. Politico, September 27, 2011.

471. Ibid.

472. *New York Times*, April 6, 2011.

473. *The Hill*, March 28, 2011.

474. Lovins and Cohen, 2011.

475. *New York Times*, April 18, 2011.

476. Heinberg, 2005.

477. Brown, 2011.

478. For example, Hansen, 2010.

479. Lovins and Cohen, 2011.

480. Ibid.

481. Skocpol and Williamson, 2011.
482. *New York Times*, October 16, 2011.
483. *The Hill*, June 20, 2013.
484. Michaels and Balling, 2009.
485. Edsall, 2012.
486. *Human Events*, April 21, 2011.
487. Helm, 2012.
488. Mooney, 2012.
489. Sherwin, 2011.
490. Shellenberger and Nordhaus, 2007.
491. Victor, 2011.
492. Mann, 2012.
493. Mooney, 2012.
494. McPherson, 2012.
495. *Forbes*, September 9, 2013
496. Einstein, 1954.
497. Leiserowitz et al., 2011.
498. Spooner and Carter, 2013.
499. Stern, 2009.
500. Shellenberger and Nordhaus, 2007.
501. McPherson, 2012.
502. Moser and Dilling, 2007.
503. Seattlepi.com, November 9, 2011.
504. International Energy Agency, 2011.
505. *New York Times*, October 16, 2011.
506. Hamilton, 2010b.
507. Parkinson, 2010.
508. McKibben, et al, 2011.
509. Gardiner, 2011.
510. Fagan, 2010.

Printed in Great Britain
by Amazon

41928013R00109